MBA
FUNDAMENTALS

BUSINESS LAW

D0745941

Kaplan MBA Fundamentals Series

MBA Fundamentals Business Law

MBA Fundamentals Statistics

From the #1 graduate test prep provider, *Kaplan MBA Fundamentals* helps you to master core business basics in a few easy steps. Each book in the series is based on an actual MBA course, providing direct and measurable skills you can use today.

For the latest titles in the series, as well as downloadable resources, visit:
www.kaplanmbafundamentals.com

MBA
FUNDAMENTALS

BUSINESS LAW

Ellen K. Curry

PUBLISHING

New York

This publication is designed to provide accurate and authoritative information in regard to the subject matter covered. It is sold with the understanding that the publisher is not engaged in rendering legal, accounting, or other professional service. If legal advice or other expert assistance is required, the services of a competent professional should be sought.

Vice President and Publisher: Maureen McMahon
Editorial Director: Jennifer Farthing
Acquisitions Editor: Shannon Berning
Development Editor: Monica P. Lugo
Production Editor: Fred Urfer
Production Designer: Pamela Beaulieu
Cover Designer: Rod Hernandez

Published by Kaplan Publishing, a division of Kaplan, Inc.
1 Liberty Plaza, 24th Floor
New York, NY 10006

Printed in the United States of America

January 2008
10 9 8 7 6 5 4 3 2 1

ISBN-13: 978-1-4277-9658-5

Kaplan Publishing books are available at special quantity discounts to use for sales promotions, employee premiums, or educational purposes. Please email our Special Sales Department to order or for more information at kaplanpublishing@kaplan.com, or write to Kaplan Publishing, 1 Liberty Plaza, 24th Floor, New York, NY 10006.

Table of Contents

Introduction

As an aspiring MBA student, an executive or professional in the work-force, or as an even everyday consumer, you come across legal issues all the time. You hear about lawsuits all the time in the nightly news. You read legal notices on product labels. Maybe you quote materials from several books in a paper you are writing a paper for class, making sure not to violate anyone's copyright. Or you agree to eBay's terms of agreement in order to become a member. You put your old baseball cards up for sale, and subsequently enter into an agreement with a guy in Seattle who wants to buy them. All of these situations have legal implications.

The purpose of this book is not to make a lawyer out of you. Whether you read it straight through or consult the sections you need for reference, this book will instead give you the basic tools you need to help you to think clearly and logically about how business and legal matters intertwine. It is also meant to aid to people who want to become more familiar with "legalese" or common legal situations, or they simply may want a "refresher course" on certain aspects of law. In fact, this book can even help you to become a better consumer and to keep you up-to-date with the global and technological realities of today's marketplace.

As you read through the day-to-day, true-to-life situations I have used as examples, you will realize that you know a lot more about this subject than you thought. Together, we will refine your critical thinking about events and we will organize concepts to make them easier to relate to and remember. I use a lot of cooking analogies to remind students that everyone starts with the basics and builds on them. In no time, with a little practice, you can be applying common recipes to interpret many business dealings.

LAW 101

Welcome to *MBA Fundamentals Business Law*. In Part I, we will start with the basics. When you begin cooking, you first learn your way around the kitchen. In "Law 101," we'll learn the basic divisions of the law and the steps that a lawsuit follows. We'll also explore some variations on the typical litigation process by reviewing methods of alternative dispute resolution. We will keep our legal analysis healthy by adding ethical considerations to our ingredients. Finally, we will see how all these elements mix with the business world.

Classifications of the Law

The law involves the most ancient of arts—storytelling. Actually, all of life's activities involve storytelling—some fiction, some nonfiction. My car starts to make a grinding sound when I start the ignition. I go to the mechanic and he translates my story into "bad spark plugs and corrosion on the cables." I get a terrible sore throat and my ears hurt. I go to the doctor and she translates my story into "strep throat, a septic bacterial infection to be treated with antibiotics." Practitioners of the law do the same thing. They label things in their own way, but they are just expressing your story in another way. Don't be too intimidated by the silly terms and ancient phrases. It is just storytelling, and you too can understand the language and translate the ideas with a little practice, patience, and common sense.

WHAT'S AHEAD

- Criminal Law
  - Misdemeanor
  - Felony
  - Standard of Proof

- Civil Law
  - Contracts
  - Torts
    - Intentional
    - Reckless
    - Negligent
  - Standard of Proof

IN THE REAL WORLD

In June 1994, Orenthal James Simpson, a.k.a O. J. Simpson, a football running back legend, was arrested and charged with the murder of his ex-wife, Nicole Brown Simpson, and a Los Angeles waiter, Ronald Goldman. Ms. Simpson and Goldman were found brutally murdered outside her home in Brentwood, California. The State of California charged Simpson with two counts of first-degree murder. One of the more bizarre aspects of the case was that before being arrested, Simpson was on the run in a famously televised car chase through the streets of L.A. A jury trial ensued. High-powered lawyers were present. And, despite the endless press analysis, the televised court sessions, the dozens of witnesses, and the incriminating car chase, Simpson was found not guilty.

Thereafter, the families of Nicole Brown Simpson and Ronald Goldman sued Simpson civilly for wrongful death. They claimed that he was responsible for the loss of their loved ones. A jury trial ensued. High-powered lawyers were present. And despite the fact that Simpson was found not guilty of the crime, he was found *liable* to the Goldman family and ordered to pay $8.5 million in *damages*. He was also found guilty of committing battery on his ex-wife, although no damages were sought by the Brown family.

How can this be? You can't be tried twice for the same crime, can you? If a criminal jury finds you not guilty—beyond a reasonable doubt—how can a civil jury punish you? And why wasn't the jig up when Simpson tried to elude the police in his Ford Bronco with a wad of cash, his passport, and a false beard?

KEY CONCEPTS

The law is a set of rules about acceptable conduct. Legal types categorize the rules that talk about conduct. The first main categories are criminal law and civil law.

Criminal Law

Criminal law regulates public standards of conduct. Each of us lives in a community, or more accurately, in layers of communities—a city, a county, a state, a nation. There are principles of conduct that your community has agreed upon, and by being a member of your community, you are held to those standards. In my community, you must drive no more than 25 miles per hour in a school zone, you cannot legally buy tobacco products until you are 18 years old, and it is against the law to break into your neighbor's house and take his property. We all agree to these rules.

If you violate a public standard of conduct, you are not always in big trouble. Sometimes a minor rule is broken. This crime is called a *misdemeanor*—and your infraction can be remedied by paying a fine or losing a *privilege*. If I linger at lunch too long, my downtown parking meter may expire, and I will get a ticket to pay. If I keep a library book too long, I cannot check out more books until I return the overdue one and pay a fine. Luckily, the law does not require you to be perfect. You can goof up quite a few times and still keep your rights and privileges, although your pocketbook may be a little lighter.

If you violate a public standard in a serious way—one that causes damage to property or injury to persons—you may have a lot to lose. When you commit a serious crime, called a *felony*, the consequences for violating the public standard of conduct could include large fines, big loss of privileges, and even the loss of your freedom to be in that society, commonly referred to as prison time. Because a felony conviction could potentially deprive a citizen of constitutionally guaranteed rights—life, liberty, and property— the stakes are very high and the law goes out of its way to get it right.

With felony charges comes a list of protections for the accused citizen, including the right to counsel, the right to trial by jury, the right to confront accusers, and the right against *self-incrimination*. Breaches of public standards of conduct are prosecuted by a public representative—the U. S. attorney, state's attorney, or county attorney—and the public pays, via their taxes, for these officials to uphold the standards that their community has set. If any fines or monetary damages are due because of violations of conduct, they are paid into the public coffers, not to individuals who may have been hurt.

You can almost always identify a criminal case by the way it is named, or *styled*, as they say in the legal world. The case will be one brought by the public against the accused, such as *U.S. v. Timothy McVeigh, State v. Simpson, People v. Larry Flynt,* or *Commonwealth v. Lizzie Borden.* The *standard of proof,* or the degree with which the charge needs to be proven against the accused in a criminal case, is *beyond a reasonable doubt,* which is the highest standard in the law. It means that the accused is presumed innocent until the *decider of fact* (the judge or the jury) believes beyond any doubt that there is no other possible explanation for what happened and who caused it. They have to be 100 percent and unanimously convinced that the person accused did what he was accused of to find criminal liability. This is another way in which the individual is protected against unfair government action.

Civil Law

The law also imposes personal responsibility on citizens in the community. This is *civil law.* The area of civil law is further divided into contract cases and tort cases. A *contract* has to do with a private promise between individuals to do something, such as provide a product, build a house, or enter into a marriage. A *tort* is a wrong you do to another person or his property. Torts are sometimes called personal injuries. It is human nature to sometimes break a promise or fail to be as careful as you should in your dealings with others. Examples of torts could be the following:

1. Joe gets drunk at a bar on Saturday night and intentionally breaks his best friend's jaw over a comment about a pool shot. An intentional injury to a citizen is quite serious. Our civil laws strive to protect citizens from this type of behavior.

2. Vice President Dick Cheney accidentally shoots his hunting partner, Harry Whittington, in the face. This is not an intentional act, but when someone is careless or reckless and bad things happen, civil law allows the injured party to recover.

3. Your neighbor takes your daughter to the swimming pool one hot afternoon with her children. She fails to keep her eye on your child every moment. Your child slips on the wet pool deck, hits her chin, and requires three stitches. This is a negligent act, but luckily, not a serious fault of your neighbor or a serious injury to your child.

There is no public *prosecutor* for these cases. Many of these cases are settled without recourse to court. If they cannot be resolved, the injured parties, called *plaintiffs*, have to hire their own lawyers and file their own lawsuits. The persons accused of violating these private standards are called *defendant*s and also hire representatives to help them tell their side of the story. If the plaintiff wins, he cannot put a defendant in jail or take away his privileges. Civil claims are all about damages, or monetary amounts, to compensate the plaintiffs for the broken promises or injuries.

The cases are brought in the parties' names, so are styled, for example, as *Smith v. Jones* or *Doe v. Wal-Mart*, or *Homeowner v. Builder* or *Credit Card Co. v. Customer*. The standard of proof, or degree with which the claim needs to be proven against a civil defendant, is a lesser standard than the criminal standard of proof. In a civil case, the plaintiff has to prove his claim by a *preponderance of the evidence*, which means that more likely than not, the defendant caused the damages that are claimed. It is not a unanimous standard, and a plaintiff can recover some damages even if there are other plausible or likely contributing factors to the situation that may have caused some harm. Sometimes the preponderance of the evidence standard is called the 51 percent rule because all the decider of fact (judge or jury) needs to find is that the defendant is more than halfway at fault in the situation.

You cannot be charged twice for the same crime. The U.S. Constitution says so in the Fifth Amendment, which forbids *double jeopardy*. But that doesn't mean that an act on your part cannot result in a number of charges. It all depends on what standards, public or private, that you violate. If you run a stop sign, you could be charged with multiple public violations: failing to stop, causing an accident, exceeding the speed limit, perhaps even failure to wear your seat belt or driving without a valid license. And all you were doing was getting a quart of milk from the corner store. In addition, your actions could have violated a private standard, to not run into others' cars, causing personal and property damage. You could then be sued civilly for damages by the owner of the car and any hurt parties. So, one action could result in a criminal and a tort charge—or several charges. Also, it could result in charges against you from many levels of government. If you rob the local bank before going for the milk, you have committed both a federal and a state crime.

THE LAW IN ACTION

O. J. Simpson was accused of two heinous crimes—breaches of public standards of conduct—that is, taking the life of two human beings. The State of California, which is where the incident occurred, brought the charges against him. The case was styled *State v. Simpson*. This was a felony charge, a serious crime, with penalties upon conviction up to and including the death penalty. The defendant was presumed innocent until proven guilty. The defendant's actions before being taken into custody were not part of the record and could not be construed as admissions of guilt. The defendant was afforded all the rights reserved to him by the law and the U.S. Constitution, including the right to a speedy trial, the right to confront his accusers, and the right to be free of incriminating himself. A trial was held where a jury of 12 citizens heard all the evidence.

The evidence presented focused on the defendant's motives and opportunities to commit the crime. It included forensic and crime scene evidence and testimony about where the defendant was during the commission of the crime. The defendant had every right to question the evidence presented and present alternate theories of what happened. One alternative theory presented was that this was a racially based case and that a detective in the case wished to frame the defendant by planting a bloody glove at the crime scene. The defendant did not take the stand in his own defense, and this fact could not be construed against him because of his Fifth Amendment right against self-incrimination. The matter of the pre-arrest flight was never brought up to the jury. It was not relevant to the homicides.

After a 133-day trial and less than four hours of jury deliberation, the defendant was found not guilty on both counts of murder and Simpson was free to go. Forever after, he would be legally not guilty of these felonious claims in the eyes of the law, although many bystanders (media, citizens) questioned the verdict. There was no appeal. The state had its chance to try the case and that was it. For better or worse, Simpson's criminal case was over.

But one act can be a crime (breach of a public standard of conduct) and also a tort (breach of a personal standard of conduct). The families of the victims sued Simpson in state court, in a case styled *Rufo v. Simpson*

(Ronald Goldman's mother's name is Sharon Rufo). The claim here was that Simpson had some involvement—51 percent or more—in the deaths of the victims and those deaths left the surviving loved ones without the support, comfort, and company of their family members. This is called a case for *wrongful death*. Here, the evidence centered on how much the victims supported and aided their families, how their deaths would result in more costs—to raise children, be without the assistance of the loved one, etc. Economic matters were at issue, not forensic findings. In this trial, the defendant's failure to testify in his own defense could be construed against him and Simpson did take the stand to deny his involvement. The fact of the *acquittal* in the criminal trial was not relevant in this trial. A jury of 12 citizens heard all the evidence in a trial lasting 41 days. After 12 hours of deliberation on the compensation issue alone, they found Simpson guilty by a preponderance of the evidence for causing the death of Ronald Goldman and ordered him to pay $8.5 million to the family for their loss. Simpson was also found guilty by a preponderance of the evidence of committing battery on his ex-wife. The Brown family did not seek damages.

Simpson was not charged twice for the same crime. He had multiple criminal charges against him, the result of one act of violence. He had multiple civil charges against him, the result of the same act. The criminal trial and the civil trial focused on entirely different evidence, and had entirely different judges presiding and juries deciding.

The potential consequences—death or lots of money—were on completely different levels. The burden of proof in each case was completely different; they do not affect each other and one does not determine the outcome of the other.

TEST YOURSELF

In 2002, Tri-State Crematory, Inc. in Noble, Georgia, was in the news. It was discovered that the business had not cremated bodies sent to them from area funeral homes. In fact, over 330 bodies were found on the 16-acre site of the business, some dating back to the early 1990s.

The state of Georgia has laws prohibiting the abusing of a corpse, laws prohibiting individuals from making false statements on death certificates, and laws prohibiting theft by deception. All these criminal violations are classified as felonies.

The crematorium had contracts with many area funeral homes to provide the cremation services for their customers. In many instances, the crematory delivered concrete mixing powder to grieving families instead of remains. Tri-State was paid for their services by the families of the deceased through the various funeral homes.

1. Could Tri-State be charged with a crime? Could they be charged with more than one crime?

2. Who would prosecute this crime?

3. What could the consequences of committing such a crime be?

4. Could anyone sue Tri-State on a civil charge? If so, who could sue and what would it be based on—a contract or a tort?

5. What could the consequences of civil liability be for Tri-State?

Brain Teaser

6. Is it easier to prove the criminal case than it is to prove the civil case?

Questions Future Chapters Will Answer

7. Could this be a federal case?

8. How can Tri-State Crematory, Inc., which is a corporation, be put in jail?

9. Could the families sue anyone other than Tri-State for their damages?

Answers can be found on pages 207–208.

KEY POINTS TO REMEMBER

- The law loves to label things. Legal terminology categorizes ideas, just like a grocery store categorizes produce and canned goods; with a road map, legal terms make sense.

- The law is all about regulating conduct among people in a community. It does not demand the best of us, but it sets minimum standards of conduct.

- Two big categories of the law are criminal law and civil law.

- Criminal law is divided into misdemeanors and felonies.

- Civil law is divided into cases involving contracts and cases involving torts.

- One act can result in both criminal and civil charges.

Civil Litigation

I have an older brother who, when asked to do chores as a teenager, would always seem to have a comment on them for my mother. This caused my mother to develop a feisty comeback of her own: "Mike, you could make a federal case out of anything." It wasn't until I got to law school that I realized my mother was wrong. You cannot make a federal case out of anything, and in this chapter you'll learn why.

WHAT'S AHEAD

- History of Civil Dispute Resolution
- Federal Court Cases
- State Court Cases of Law and Equity

- Sources of the Law
- Steps in a Lawsuit

IN THE REAL WORLD

In 2005, Acme Construction Company, located in Davenport, Scott County, Iowa, signed a contract to do a commercial build-out just across the Mississippi River. They were constructing a new Bijou Jewelry for Jim and Jerry Ballard, who were expanding from their small family store in Cambridge,

Henry County, Illinois, to the new King Mall in Moline, Rock Island County, Illinois, which is about 20 miles away. The Ballards wanted a glitzy store worthy of the big city and the new mall, complete with custom-built display cases and flashy lighting. Acme had been recommended by business contacts and gave an affordable estimate and workable timetable. Work proceeded, and, as is common, changes were made. The Ballards asked for more display areas than first bid and for some upgrades in finish materials, like the granite on the walls and floor. Some of these change orders were reduced to writing, some were not.

The additions to the contract took more time to complete, so when May 1 came, the store was not ready for the grand opening that was planned and highly anticipated. Acme put in overtime and Bijou had a sparkly, albeit sparsely attended, opening on May 8. Acme sent the final bill to the Ballards for $22,000 on May 10, having already received $60,000 in progress payments. On May 11, the Ballards told Acme that due to the late opening, the absence of an agreement to pay overtime, and the cost overruns, they were not paying one more dime.

Before either party runs to the courthouse, Acme and the Ballards try to resolve their dispute. Acme is reluctant to sue because this job was recommended by other Acme customers and word would get back to them. Plus, there is a lot of interest in Acme's talents by other mall stores, including one of the big anchor stores. However, the $22,000 balance already reflects some concessions to Bijou for the job timing. In addition, the Ballards made the changes, not Acme. The Ballards are nervous because they have already expended their budget for the mall location and the grand opening was lightly attended. They may have to go to the bank for some extra working capital and don't want to look foolish about their expansion or tardy in their bill paying. After some initial discussion, neither party is happy. Does either party have a cause of action they could take to court? Where should the lawsuit be filed?

KEY CONCEPTS

Generally, when a person commits a misdemeanor, she pays the fine and it is over. Often, even more serious crimes, like failing to stop at a light, are resolved with a fine, loss of driving privileges, or a course at driving school. There is an accident in the store parking lot. More than likely, the parties will exchange information, insurance companies will be contacted, and the matter will be resolved through business channels.

We even hear about public prosecutors accepting negotiated settlements in serious criminal matters. In fact, it is estimated that 85 to 90 percent of criminal matters never result in a trial and approximately 95 percent of civil matters settle by agreement. However, some cases are not settled, and if the parties feel that a public or private standard has been violated and the actor must be punished, the recourse in this country is to take your cause of action (case) to court.

History of Civil Dispute Resolution

The handling of disputes wasn't always that way. In ancient times, it was often the officials of society, frequently religious leaders, who resolved disputes, many times with a trial by torture to test if the wrongdoer was evil or untruthful. If the accused recovered after the torture, he was exonerated. The American law system is based on the English system. In medieval times, disputes were settled with a *trial by ordeal*. The accused would undergo some awful exercise involving a hot poker or boiling water or poisonous potions, and if he came out alive, it was determined that God was on his side and he was truthful. Then often, the accuser was punished.

Among the aristocrats, there was a more civilized way of dispute resolution, called *trial by combat* or *judicial duel*. This was also an accusatory procedure, and the accused was duty bound to defend his honor by fighting to prove truthfulness. Again, God was the judge. Some nobles were better fighters than others, and over time, it was agreed that you could hire an *advocatus* (advocate—usually a knight) to defend for you. This helped the survival rate among peers, but still was not the best way to solve disputes.

In the later Middle Ages, *trial by oath* became popular. In this system, the parties would need to prove their claims by collecting oaths or sworn statements supporting them from lords, peers, or others of high estate. The party with the best backup won. Again, advocates were used to help *litigators* through the system, but in this case their weapons were oratory skills and knowledge of the law. The accuser and accused could not testify themselves about their own matter, as it was assumed they would lie. A jury from the community (of their peers) usually determined the outcome.

The system has continued to evolve, but the basics are recognizable back to the Middle Ages. Today, if you have a dispute to settle and must go to court, you first need to decide what court to go to. There are 51 major court systems in the United States—the federal court system and 50 state court systems. Each has its own rules about what it does. But you cannot make a federal case out of everything. You cannot take a matter about divorce to small claims court nor can you take a traffic citation to probate court. Depending on the nature of the case, the parties involved, and the amount of money at issue, there is a right court for every dispute.

Federal Court Cases

To get into federal court, you must be charged with a federal crime or have an eligible civil case. In addition, federal courts will hear any dispute involving the Constitution of the United States. Interstate kidnapping and bank robbery are crimes that violate federal law and go to federal court. Cases involving civil rights or a freedom guaranteed in the Bill of Rights go to federal court. Your fender bender usually does not. The reason is *judicial economy*. The federal courts want to take the most important cases they can and cases that may not be fairly heard in other jurisdictions. To get your civil dispute in federal court, you need to have a federal issue, a federal crime, a matter between states or between a state of the United States and a foreign country, or a matter that qualifies for *diversity jurisdiction*.

Diversity jurisdiction is how most private claimants get to federal court. It means that the *plaintiffs* (those suing) need to live in a state different from the *defendants* (those being sued). Federal courts figure, if you both live in Iowa, you can go to Iowa to resolve your dispute. But if a party lives in California, and was hit by my car while on vacation in Iowa, it may not be fair for me to go to San Luis Obispo or for them to come to Davenport, Iowa, and be judged by a jury of locals with local sympathies and ethics. In addition, just so the workload doesn't get too petty, to qualify for federal diversity jurisdiction the parties must have at least $75,000 in dispute.

Once it is decided that you will seek a public solution to your dispute, you have to decide where to go. That is a question of *jurisdiction*. There are 51 main jurisdictions and many subjurisdictions within the United States. If you have a federal matter, you check a map and see which federal district you are in. The country is divided into 11 sections, or federal court *districts*, and you file your federal case in the closest courthouse to where you reside, where the defendants reside, or where the accident happened. Often, local federal court districts have offices in your nearest federal building. States also have divided their court systems into districts, sometimes called *circuits*, to give a *litigant* as local a place as possible to conduct his trial. County seats are often where state district courthouses or circuit courthouses are located. It is also common for courts to be divided further by the matters they hear. Your local courthouse may have a small claims division (for claims that involve low dollar amounts and where litigants can argue their own cases without lawyers), traffic divisions, juvenile courts, family courts, probate courts (for wills and estate matters), and district courts for everything else. You have to evaluate what you are asking for to know which court to go to.

State Court Cases of Law and Equity

Sometimes state courts are divided into law and equity divisions. This is also a throwback to medieval English legal tradition. The realm used to belong to the sovereign—the king. He granted estates and honors to fellow nobles, but he could take them away. When disputes between lords and peers arose, the king was the arbiter of disputes, since it was all about him anyway. Over time, the king didn't want to always hold court listening to complaints. He had better things to do, so he delegated the decision-making in court to his lords. They could decide disputes based on the king's directions—the statements he had made before.

Sometimes claimants came to court and asked for something that didn't fit the mold. They didn't want an injury paid for or a bill resolved, they wanted the court to decide an issue of fairness, called *equity*. They asked the court to order someone to marry someone else or to turn over a shipment of grain. This left the lords a little confused. There were no clear directions about fairness and it wasn't even certain they were qualified to rule on these questions. The king set up a separate court system; now the people could seek recourse in the law court or in equity court, and in equity the lords would apply principles of fairness and evenhanded dealing.

In the United States, we adopted this law and equity tradition, but today the law and equity courts are joined. When you go to your county courthouse or your federal courthouse to file a case, you can combine requests for legal and equitable decisions in one filing. An example might be in a divorce case, where there is not only a legal ruling ending the marital status, but also an equitable ruling keeping the parties from harassing each other at their respective homes.

So, how do you know which court to go to? You consider your matter. Is it a federal case? If not, what state court could you go to? This depends on where the plaintiff resides, where the defendant resides, and where the incident that is the subject of the lawsuit took place. Sometimes there is only one answer, sometimes there are a few choices. How do you choose? This is a strategic point that your legal advisors consider, weighing your litigation budget, timing, and type of matter. It is cheaper to try a case in Kansas than it is in California. You also get a quicker hearing date because the court calendar is not so full. However, Kansas jurors are traditionally not as generous in their monetary awards as those liberal Californians. Also, if most of your witnesses and medical experts are in Kansas, you have to consider the cost of getting them to California to testify. Finally, as if these aren't enough choices, different laws apply in Kansas than in California, and those laws could have a dramatic influence on the outcome of your case.

Sources of the Law

Since there are 51 court systems in this country, there are 51 different sets of laws that could be applied to your case. Where do the courts look to decide your matter? First, they look to the U.S. Constitution, which is the supreme law of the land. No other law that the federal government or any state government passes can conflict with the U.S. Constitution. Next, each court system looks to the laws passed by the legislature of that jurisdiction. Federal courts look at laws passed by Congress. State courts look at state laws, often compiled into *codes*, such as the Iowa Code, or statute books, such as Illinois Compiled Statutes. Finally, if neither the U.S. Constitution nor federal or state laws give guidance on the issue before the court, the court could look to the former case law, called *common law*, to decide a situation. In our country, we like predictability in the law, so if you can find a previous case with similar facts as yours that went to court and received a ruling from a judge or a jury, you can rely on that outcome to predict what will happen in your case. This is called a *precedent*. Courts must observe what went before and be in conformance with it. This is also called the doctrine of *stare decisis,* which means "let the previous ruling stand."

Some states allow same-sex unions, some states grant liberal child support, and some states have low tax rates for corporations. Depending on what you want a court to consider for you, you may be able to predict a better outcome in one jurisdiction over another. If you bring your fender bender case in Kansas, that state's tort law will apply. If you bring your case in California, you may be able to predict a bigger award for pain and suffering than in Kansas. These laws that have to do with the subject matter of the case are called *substantive laws*. There are 51 sets of substantive laws in the United States; many are the same state to state, many are different. Each jurisdiction also has some laws that relate to how to try a case; these are called *procedural laws*. For example, in Iowa, if you are served with notice that someone is suing you, you have 20 days to respond to the lawsuit. In Illinois, you have 30 days. These are examples of procedural rules, as are statutes of limitations, rules for witness testimony, and number of copies of documents you must file with the court. Each jurisdiction has its own procedural rules.

Now comes the tricky part: What if there is no federal law about the substance or subject of your case and you are in federal court? Sure, there are federal criminal laws, but there is no federal substantive corporation law—incorporating is governed by each state. In that case, the federal court applies the substantive law of the state in which they are sitting. So, a federal judge sitting in Kansas may spend a lot of his day applying Kansas state substantive law and federal procedural law to the cases at hand. Luckily, the sophisticated strategy of court jurisdiction is a matter for the lawyers. What is good to note, though, is that depending on where you do business, you may be subject to laws of another jurisdiction and those different rules could have a significant impact on the outcome of your dispute.

Steps in a Lawsuit

Whether you bring your claim in federal or state court, there is a predictable step-by-step process of pursuing a lawsuit. First, you file a *complaint*, sometimes called a *pleading*. This seems appropriate since you are bringing up something you are complaining about and you are pleading for help to resolve it. The filer of a complaint is called the plaintiff or the *petitioner*, since you are being plaintive with the court and asking for (petitioning for) relief. The papers you file are served on the person you are arguing with, called the defendant (defending himself against your charges). Sometimes the defendant is called the *respondent* (because he is responding to your complaint and it sounds more neutral than to call him the defendant, which implies guilt). The defendant can answer the claim and even bring his own claim against the plaintiff in the same case. The idea of judicial economy is that if you are going to court, you may as well air all the issues between you to save court time and resources, so often a plaintiff gets countersued by the defendant on the theory of "if I have to be there anyway...." The defendant can even bring in parties that the plaintiff didn't originally include in the suit, by way of a *cross-claim*. The defendant will do this also for judicial economy. If the defense argues that they are not liable to the plaintiff because someone else was to blame for the incident, that someone else may as well be there to get this all worked out. These pleadings sent back and forth can take months to exchange. All the claims have to be stated and responded to between all the parties involved. If there are multiple plaintiffs and/or multiple defendants, the pleading process can be quite complex.

Next, there is a process of discovery that takes place between the parties. *Discovery* is the process of gathering the relevant evidence to prove your case. It could include taking written or oral statements and gathering witnesses, diagrams, tests, expert testimony, or scientific research on the issue. This step is costly and time consuming, but it helps the parties clarify where they each stand and the veracity of the claims being made. Many cases settle at some point during the discovery process because the parties more clearly view their respective positions and cut their losses. *Interrogatories* (written questions and answers between parties) and *depositions* (sworn statements by parties and witnesses) are used widely in discovery.

When discovery is nearing completion, a trial date is usually set, which can easily be two years or more from the date the case was filed depending on the jurisdiction. At trial, the parties each get a chance to do their storytelling—with testimony, exhibits, and cross-examination—to attempt to convince the *trier of fact*, who is a judge or a jury, of what happened. Whoever tells the most believable story wins. In a civil case, if the plaintiff wins, she gets a judgment for damages in an amount that the court determines. If the plaintiff loses, the defendant just has to pay his attorney for defending him.

If one side is unhappy with the result of the trial, it is possible, but not a guaranteed right, to *appeal* the judgment to a higher court, which is a U.S. court of appeals or a state *appellate court*. The appellate court does not retry the case. They do not hear the witnesses again; they do not view the exhibits. In our system, the trial court determines the facts of a case because the trial court sees it all—the witnesses, the reactions, the exhibits. They make a finding of fact that sticks with the case forever. What is appealed is a point of law or a procedural point about the trial. If the trial court misapplied the law in question, the appellate court may reverse the ruling. If a piece of evidence that the appellate court felt was procedurally necessary was not allowed in at the trial, the trial court ruling could be changed. The facts are never changed on appeal.

So you have one shot to get it right. If you cannot prove O. J. Simpson guilty beyond a reasonable doubt to the jury of his peers at trial, you cannot have another chance to prove your case. Simpson is forever not a murderer of Nicole Brown Simpson or Ronald Goldman.

THE LAW IN ACTION

Despite the fact that filing a lawsuit could ruin business relationships, generate bad publicity, and cost thousands of dollars in legal fees, $22,000 is too much for Acme to lose and too much for the Ballards to pay. Either party could file a lawsuit. It doesn't matter in a civil action who is the plaintiff. It does not mean you are the good guy. Being the defendant does not mean you are the bad guy. If Acme sues the Ballards to collect money due under the construction contract, the Ballards will certainly countersue Acme for overcharging without change orders and failing to meet the opening date. If the Ballards sue on the theory of breach of contract, so the contract amount is reduced and the contract is considered paid in full, Acme will certainly countersue for all the pricey marble and the labor to install it.

The lawsuit could be filed in Scott County, Iowa, where Acme does business and where the contract was entered into, or it could be filed in Henry County, Illinois, where the Ballards live and still operate their first store. The lawsuit could also be filed in Rock Island County, Illinois, where the work was done. Although the case could have been filed in federal court if no money was paid along the way, it cannot be filed there now. The requirements for federal diversity jurisdiction are plaintiffs having different citizenship from defendants (which is true here) and more than $75,000 at issue (which is not true due to the progress payments).

When more than one court has jurisdiction over a dispute, it is called *concurrent jurisdiction*. Here both Iowa and Illinois have jurisdiction, or a court that could "speak the law" to the parties about this dispute. Whoever files first determines where the dispute will be resolved. The other party cannot defend in one state and file a countersuit in another. When considering the choice in this case, the parties would weigh the costs of filing in each location, the timing for getting a matter to trial, the location of the witnesses and interested parties needing to be present at trial, the average award amounts made on contract dispute cases in each jurisdiction, and the substantive law to be applied. If Iowa had rules that were more lenient on contract change orders, Acme would want to be there. If Illinois had more contract cases that interpreted timing in contracts as critical, the Ballards would want to be there.

TEST YOURSELF

The winter of 2006 was quite cold in Galesburg, Illinois. The Lynch family used a portable kerosene heater in their basement to help keep warm. One Sunday afternoon, when Mr. and Mrs. Lynch were watching television in the basement with their twin daughters, their boys—Sam and Dan—filled the heater in the utility room. They overfilled the unit and the extra kerosene caught fire as it splashed against the hot metal, causing an immediate fireball and explosion. Only Mr. Lynch, 39, and Sam, 13, made it out alive. Sam has severe burns. Mrs. Lynch, 39, the twin girls, 7, and Dan, 10, all perished in the fire. The house is a total loss. The heater was manufactured by Heat-all Industries, headquartered in Estes, Minnesota. The Lynches purchased the heater from the local Sears store three months ago.

1. Does Mr. Lynch or Sam have a cause of action to pursue?

2. Is this case based on a contract or a tort?

3. Who would be the defendant(s) in this case?

4. In what state(s) could a lawsuit be sought?

5. Can this case be filed in federal court? In state court? In more than one state court?

Brain Teaser

6. If you had the choice to go to federal court or state court with this case and you knew that federal juries were very conservative in awarding damages in death cases but state juries in Chicago were very liberal, which court would you choose to file in?

Questions Future Chapters Will Answer

7. When does the location of a corporation's headquarters come into play?

8. When a case is as serious and complex as this one, is it mandatory to have a trial?

Answers can be found on pages 208–210.

KEY POINTS TO REMEMBER

- When a person commits a crime or a civil violation, the first step for the injured party is to try to work to a conclusion by agreement or negotiation.

- If a matter cannot be resolved through private agreement, the injured party may seek recourse in a court of law; in other words, you have a cause of action.

- Depending on the type of matter, the parties involved, and the amount of damages at issue, there is a right court for you. Deciding which is the right court is a matter of jurisdiction.

- There are 51 major court systems in the United States—1 federal and 50 state systems.

- All courts decide cases by looking at the law, which comes from the U.S. Constitution, statutes, and past case decisions, called common law.

- When litigating, the court applies substantive laws (about what type of case you have) and procedural laws (about how to go about the court proceeding).

- The steps in a lawsuit take time and resources—but each step makes sense and keeps the process as orderly as possible.

- If you don't like your trial court result, you may be able to appeal your case, but an appeal is not a new trial.

Alternative Dispute Resolution

My husband tells a great story about compromise. When his mother let him and his younger brother have a candy bar, one son would get to cut the candy bar into two pieces and the other son would get to choose which piece he wanted. This at least appeared to promote fairness with minimal squabbling. Everyone got a little of what they wanted.

This chapter is about alternatives to litigation as methods of dispute resolution, or a kinder, gentler way to resolve disputes so that everyone can get a little of what they want.

WHAT'S AHEAD

• Negotiation	• Arbitration
• Mediation	

IN THE REAL WORLD

The dispute discussed in chapter 2 between Acme Construction Co. and Jim and Jerry Ballard is a good example of a case that may benefit from some *alternative dispute resolution* (ADR). The parties are disputing the remaining contract balance of $22,000 that Acme demanded, but the

Ballards refused to pay because of estimate overruns and delays with the store project in King Mall. The parties are at an impasse: neither wants to throw out a figure, but the difference is too great to walk away. In chapter 2, some complications were discussed about where a lawsuit could be filed, how long it may take, and what resources it may cost before there is any solution for either side. In this case, the parties may benefit by trying to negotiate, mediate, or arbitrate this matter to a conclusion.

KEY CONCEPTS

Alternative dispute resolution has been around for a long time. It was popular in medieval England because it allowed for parties to be appeased without resorting to the humiliating and sometimes deadly outcomes of trials by combat described in chapter 2. There were many informal pressures to compromise, especially among merchants who needed to continue doing business with each other in small towns. There were family pressures put upon arguing parties, and the possibility of being shunned in your own community was a strong deterrent to a sustained argument. In fact, resolutions of disputes made outside of the courtroom were so frequent that the populace had their own word for a mediated settlement. It was a *loveday*. I doubt that YouTube and the record industry are going to have a loveday soon, but there is good reason for disputing parties to try to avoid a prolonged court fight.

Most disputes today are settled without trials. Some matters get settled before there ever is the need to consider filing a lawsuit. Some get settled after a lawsuit is filed, but before the parties go so far into it as to have totally prepared for trial and set a date.

There are many factors that determine if a dispute will be settled outside of court or with a trial. Usually small matters that can be ignored or disagreements involving small amounts of money just fade away. When a matter is too serious to be ignored, the parties still must weigh the time involved in pursuing a legal remedy, the costs, the energy that goes into a legal resolution, and the publicity a court matter will generate. In addition, when a matter goes to court, there is usually a declared winner and a declared loser. No one wants to be a loser.

Negotiation

The simplest and most common alternative to a court case is for the parties to negotiate. *Negotiation* can take many forms, from a very informal meeting over coffee to a roundtable discussion with attorneys present on each side. However, it is voluntary, so both sides must agree to try it. The purpose of a negotiation is to talk freely about making a deal.

There is usually a lot of psychology involved in business disputes, even if you think of them just in terms of numbers and facts. Sometimes just the opportunity for each side to air its point or agree to disagree is helpful to ending the stalemate and moving on. Negotiation is widely used in employment matters, especially with unions, about job performance and complaints. Having a set routine for handling these matters takes the personal element out of the equation, or at least minimizes it. Negotiation is also used between businesses that have a continuing relationship. No one wants a misdirected delivery of 100 No. 2 pencils to terminate a business relationship between customer and supplier worth thousands of dollars a year.

Negotiation is increasingly popular in other civil matters, such as marital, child custody, and support disputes. Often sitting down with an agenda and attorneys as witnesses helps people who cannot have a civil conversation on their own. Matters are taken one by one, and each party has a chance to talk. This leads to less blaming and more results.

In negotiation, there is no requirement to come to a result. Many times a conclusion is not reached, or at least, not at first, but the airing of the issues is a good step in the process. Each party comes away from the experience with a better idea of where they stand, and the experience may spur a later resolution before trial.

Mediation

Mediation is a bit more complex than negotiation because it involves a third party—the mediator. Mediation still has to be voluntary, so both sides of the dispute must agree to try mediation, but this time, they do it in front of a master of ceremonies. The *mediator* is a neutral party present to help the sides discuss their issues, but also to take an active role by suggesting solutions, compromises, or bargains that may facilitate a settlement. The parties can have their attorneys with them at mediation, but the mediator is in charge.

Often mediation will start with each side telling their story to the other side and the mediator. After this, the mediator may split up the sides to the dispute and talk to one party about the strengths and weaknesses of their argument and press them for their settlement range. Then, that side will be escorted to the waiting room while the mediator "beats up" on the other side. This is a chance for each party to get a neutral reaction to their case. This is different from the plaintiff's management telling them what a good position they are in or their attorneys telling them that the case is strong; rather, this may be the first "outside" voice they have gotten, and sometimes it is a surprise. Not everyone sees matters as the litigants do. Not everyone gets as emotional and incensed as the parties to a lawsuit. It is a great leveler.

Sessions may go back and forth for a while, joint meetings may be had again; the process will go along as long as the mediator feels it is helpful. As with negotiation, there is no requirement to reach a settlement. But settlement or no, the process and the feedback gained from the session can be very helpful to the realistic assessment of the case at hand.

Mediators are chosen by the parties and should be neutral or independent. They may be chosen for their legal expertise. Many mediators are attorneys or retired judges. Some mediators are chosen for their knowledge in the field. For example, in a medical malpractice case, perhaps a physician would serve as a mediator. In a construction case, an engineer or architect may be the best judge of what is going on. There are many sources to locate mediators, among them bar associations and arbitration and mediation groups. The parties to the dispute usually agree on how to pay the mediator, whose fees are not based on the outcome of the case (naturally), but are generally an hourly or daily rate. Many employment contracts call for disputes to be mediated, as do many supplier contracts, construction matters, consumer purchases, and even billing disputes.

Like negotiation, mediation can be accomplished faster than a trial. Depending on the jurisdiction involved, getting a case to trial could take between two and five years. You could agree to negotiate next week or find a mediator for 10 days from now. Both negotiation and mediation are cheaper than a trial because they are less formal. You do not have to develop your evidence as strictly as with a court trial. You may choose to have fewer witnesses and experts to present to a mediator than you would to a judge or jury. It is a less threatening and forbidding setting than a courthouse, so parties often are more at ease and better at telling their stories than in front of a judge, jury, court reporter, and gallery. And like negotiation, mediation can be empowering to the parties. They have a say in the solution to the problem. They can mold the compromise to include some points that are really important to their feeling good about the outcome—or if not good, at least not victimized.

Many state and federal courts are requiring parties to a lawsuit to have a mandatory settlement conference during the pendency of the case. Even if prior discussions have been unsuccessful, this forced, court-ordered, sit-down meeting resolves many disputes and frees up valuable court time.

Arbitration

Arbitration is the most formal of the alternative dispute resolution formats. This process uses a neutral third party or, on occasion, neutral third parties or panels. Arbitration is voluntary, so both parties must agree to resort to this technique. Arbitrators are found through bar associations or arbitration and mediation groups and reflect the expertise needed to consider the subject at issue. The parties to the dispute can agree to make the arbitration binding, which means whatever result the arbitrator or arbitrators come up with will end the matter. *Binding arbitration* means agreeing to let the arbitrator be the judge in your case.

The parties can also agree to *nonbinding arbitration*. But why go through the whole process and get a "decision" from the arbitrator if no one is bound by it? Because even though nonbinding arbitration may not end a case, it still gives the parties a dry run of their trial. They get feedback and a more realistic idea of the strength of their case by having arbitrated. If the parties want to hedge their bets, they can agree to nonbinding arbitration and if they both like the decision, they can agree to make it binding. Because arbitration is more formal and complex than mediation or negotiation, it can be costly. In some cases, it is as costly as going to trial, but still preferred because it is more private than a public trial and the rules of evidence are more relaxed than in court.

Today, there is wide use of ADR clauses in contracts. Employers may require employees to mediate a work dispute, union members may have to arbitrate their work condition, suppliers may contractually have to mediate disputes with clients, and customers may have to mediate with auto companies to get their "lemon" cars repaired. When parties agree to use ADR, they give up a constitutionally guaranteed right to seek redress of their grievances in court. This is an important right for citizens and businesses. The issue has been raised whether contracts that require ADR are constitutional. In other words, do you have to settle your matter as the contract says, or could you go directly to court and sue over your disagreement? The law has upheld ADR contract terms so long as the parties to the contract are clearly aware of these terms at the signing of the agreement.

Alternative dispute resolution is here to stay. Its use grows every year, and new forms of negotiating settlements are being developed in the law and in private industry. One reason for its popularity is that the parties really have nothing to lose. The fact that ADR has taken place, and any offers of settlement that were made in an ADR negotiation, are not admissible if the matter eventually goes to trial. It is a way for parties to a dispute to get on with what they do best—running their businesses rather than being mired in a lawsuit with all its expenditures of money, time, and energy. It is also a way for the parties to be part of the solution to the problem. If the court determines the facts of the case, those are the facts forever after; there is a winner and a loser. ADR is a way to resolve disputes so everyone gets a little of what they want.

THE LAW IN ACTION

Could Acme Construction resolve the $22,000 issue with the Ballards without going to trial? Sure they could, but they may need some help. Before this case would even be filed, the parties would probably try to negotiate a settlement through their attorneys. Maybe they are so emotional and scared right now that this will go nowhere. Neither party may be willing to start the bidding.

Perhaps agreeing on a neutral third party could be successful. A mediator in the construction industry might be able to evaluate the reasonableness of the overtime and material costs as well as the degree of difficulty the change orders added to the job.

An outside commercial attorney or retired judge may evaluate the strength of the legal arguments to persuade the parties to come to a settlement. Mediation could occur relatively quickly, or after some of the discovery has taken place. Witnesses including the Ballards and the construction supervisor and crew could appear in a casual setting and give their information informally. The mediator could ask them direct questions to get all the details that are important. The mediator could "lean on" each side to make some compromises in amounts, but also on equitable or fairness questions. Perhaps the Ballards could have 90 days to pay the balance due giving them a period of time to see how popular the new store becomes; perhaps they could have the remaining marble not used on the job. A mediator familiar with the complications of change orders could explain to the Ballards that their extra cabinets and upgrades could not reasonably have been done on the same timetable. Maybe that mediator could impress upon Acme that they were in a superior position to know there would be a timing problem and should have explained this better to the customer. By chance, there could be some punch list items left to complete and the Ballards might be worried that Acme won't complete them unless the entire bill is paid. With mediation, each party could express what is really important to them, establish what their settlement range is, and get a little something they want. There would be no winner or loser.

But maybe each party is entrenched in their position. The matter may be at a stalemate—$22,000 on one side and not a dime on the other. Binding arbitration could settle the matter more quickly and cheaply than a trial. Each side would have input into the selection of the arbitrator or arbitrators, unlike in a trial, where you take the judge you get or work with the jury pool you have. Arbitration would be less public. The Ballards don't want the main chapter in their expansion history to be about a bill dispute. Acme wants to do more business in the mall. They both want to get on with what they do best—construction and sales. Much like a judge, an arbitrator could weigh the matter and present a workout, which is what in effect the court would do at trial. The arbitrator might take solution suggestions from both sides so the parties could live with the outcome. Again, there would be no winner or loser.

TEST YOURSELF

Dog's Best Friend Co. is a manufacturer of dog food that is sold to three leading dog food companies for distribution under their own labels. Last month, a shipment of ingredients from the Far East contained a contaminant that was mixed into canned dog food distributed in 10 states. Before the contamination was discovered, 22 dogs in eight states fell seriously ill with kidney failure. Fifteen dogs died. The manufacturer immediately issued a recall of all cans distributed, but more cases of ailing dogs are being reported each day.

Review Questions

1. Do the pet owners have a cause of action (case) against the manufacturer of the dog food? Is it based on a contract or a tort?

2. Dog's Best Friend Co. is located in California, but all the contaminated food was delivered to Midwest and southern states. Since no contaminated food got to consumers in California, the company feels it is safe from any lawsuits. Do you agree?

3. In the worst case scenario, Dog's Best Friend president, Mr. Hound, feels the company might have to reimburse customers for the cost of the bad dog food. Is Mr. Hound correct?

Test Yourself on This Chapter

4. List three reasons why Dog's Best Friend should consider using ADR to resolve claims about contaminated dog food.

5. What kind of experience should a mediator in this case have? Why?

Brain Teaser

6. What could be some creative and equitable points to include in a negotiated settlement that would make the manufacturer look better and the victims feel better?

Question Future Chapters Will Answer

7. Isn't there a law that products should be fit for their purpose? Where was the FDA?

Answers can be found on pages 210–211.

KEY POINTS TO REMEMBER

- Alternative dispute resolution (ADR), which is growing in popularity, is used to resolve business and personal litigation matters quickly, cheaply, informally, and more privately than litigation.

- Alternative dispute resolution options include negotiation, mediation, and arbitration.

- In business, there is a big advantage to resolving disputes at the cheapest, quickest level and getting on with what you do best—more business.

- ADR allows the parties, rather than a judge or jury, to decide what is most important to them, and it allows for more equitable and ethical considerations in outcomes.

- Negotiation allows the parties to get together, either personally or with an advocate, to discuss the issues involved and to work out the dispute.

- Mediation uses a third party to direct the discussions between the parties, trying to get each side to see the strengths and weaknesses of their position, with the goal of moderating a mutually acceptable solution to the issues.

- Arbitration is the use of a third party or parties that consider presentations from each side and make a determination on how the issues should be resolved. Arbitration can be binding or nonbinding on the parties to the dispute.
- Even if ADR fails to conclude a dispute, the process gives the parties a more realistic idea of their arguments and possible outcomes.
- The fact that ADR has taken place, and any offers of settlement made during any ADR, are not admissible pieces of information at trial if the parties fail to reach a negotiated resolution of the case.

Ethics and the Law

E thics is the study of right behavior or how people should act. In Victorian times, it was unheard of for a single lady to be in a man's presence unchaperoned. If she found herself in that situation, her reputation was ruined. In Victorian times, many a gentleman engaged in buying and selling human beings as slaves. If he found himself in that business, his reputation was made.

Times change and ethics change. Even in the same time frame, in the same culture, ethics collide. In this chapter, we will discuss the relationship between what is legal and what is ethical. As we discussed earlier, the law does not require perfect behavior. In reality, it sets minimal standards of conduct. Ethics, on the other hand, is about goodness and ideals. A legal act, such as choosing not to recycle, could well be wrong conduct according to your conscience. But an ethical act for you, such as composting all your garbage in your backyard, which is in city limits, could be illegal. In this chapter, we will discuss some of the influences on legal and ethical decision-making. We will also discuss how your business decisions involving ethics can ruin or make your reputation.

WHAT'S AHEAD

- Businesses and Legality
- Theories of Ethical Behavior
- Businesses and Ethics
- Stakeholders to Consider
- If it's legal, is it ethical? If it's ethical, is it legal?

IN THE REAL WORLD

In 1951, a Davenport, Iowa, artist started a small sculpture business. Isabel Bloom had studied art with Grant Wood at the Stone City Art Colony in the 1930s. Her style was thoroughly American, realistic, and tied to the heartland. Her sculptures were made from Mississippi River clay and concrete, lovingly hand-finished in the shape of rabbits, owls, hedgehogs, and roly-poly children, then finished with a greenish hand-rubbing and signed by the artist. The small business was a local fixture for years and a source of authentic prairie gifts for travelers and natives. The sculptures were moderately priced and therefore popular birthday, graduation, wedding, and anniversary presents.

As Isabel entered her eighties, she sold the business, Isabel Bloom, Ltd., to three local businessmen. They continued to run the operation from its Village of East Davenport location overlooking the river; but they also expanded production and started distributing the sculptures to Midwestern gift stores, including stores in Chicago suburbs. Sales grew. The handmade techniques continued until early 2006, when the owners announced that the production of Isabel Bloom statues would be moved to China. The move would mean lower production costs and better distribution possibilities in the United States. The move would also mean the loss of 50 jobs in Davenport and no more hand-finishing or Mississippi River clay. The items would still be signed ISABEL BLOOM on the bottom. It was purely a business decision.

KEY CONCEPTS

The discipline of ethics concerns the study of what is considered good and bad behavior. The discipline of running a business concerns making a profit. Ethical principles and business principles are both affected by the times in which they operate and by the traditions they have known, yet in the end, a business is good when it is profitable and bad when it is not.

Businesses and Legality

To be profitable, most businesses observe the law. There is a definite and usually swift consequence for violating a public or private standard of conduct. With a criminal violation, a company may be charged a monetary fine, which certainly impacts the bottom line. A criminal penalty could also include a loss of license or privilege, which would affect future profits. If a business breaches a contract, a civil violation has occurred, which could result in the company having to compensate the damaged party with money. If a business commits a tort—injuring someone or damaging his property—the law will require the business to put the injured party back in the position he was in before the tort occurred, which again could mean significant compensation going to the victim. Therefore, businesses try to refrain from committing illegal acts.

Businesses are not only expected to operate legally, they are also expected to operate ethically. However, what is right behavior for some is not right behavior for others. Individuals' ethical sensibilities differ wildly, and so do those of businesses. In the long run, a failure to be aware of and sensitive to ethical concerns can affect a business's profit as much as an illegal act can. The public responds to ethical concerns, and even though a business may be operating within the law, if it makes poor ethical choices for its times and audience, it will lose profits and thereby be off purpose.

Theories of Ethical Behavior

Ethics are nebulous—often as cloudy as the Milky Way. Philosophers have labeled some basic theories about ethical behavior. For example, one widely recognized ethical theory is the *principle of utility*. A utilitarian makes decisions of right and wrong focusing on the outcome that provides the greatest good for the greatest number of people. Another ethical theory is the *principle of egoism*. An ethical egoist would not care a bit how a decision affected another; he values whatever is in his own best interest, and by definition, that must be the best choice. Someone who believes in the principle of the *categorical imperative* would say that a decision is a right one if he is willing to have the same decision imposed upon him. In other words, a believer in the categorical imperative would consider it ethical to lie to another if he agrees that anyone else can lie to him. These are just three ethical theories out of many. People in all places and at all times have disagreed about what is right behavior. One ethical theory is not superior to another, just different from it.

Businesses and Ethics

When an ethical question arises, how can a business, whose main goal is to make a profit, get it right? The simple answer is that a business cannot get it right all the time. There will always be an audience that disagrees with its decisions. However, a business's ethical choices can affect profits just as seriously as illegal choices. For example, Wal-Mart, the world's largest retailer, continually gets feedback on its choices. Locking employees in at the workplace is a bad choice. Offering personal wellness programs is a good choice. Nike uses celebrities to promote their sports shoes. This is good choice. Nike uses Indonesian manufacturing facilities with poor working conditions. That is a bad choice. Alcoa is the leading manufacturer of aluminum. Manufacturing aluminum creates some serious environmental by-products. Alcoa chooses to sponsor many environmental causes and education programs. This is probably a deliberate choice to enhance the company's reputation as a good neighbor and an environmentally responsible organization.

To guide them in making ethical choices, many businesses adopt ethical codes, *mission statements*, or statements of purpose. These pronouncements give some insight into the values of a company. Also, a company can be evaluated for its good or bad behavior by looking at its choices of wage levels and the fringe benefits it offers employees, its hours of operation, or its company morale and community involvement.

If the reaction to a business decision is extremely negative, the company may change its choice. If a business's choices are considered serious violations of ethical standards, the issue may be addressed by the public or legislature, resulting in steps to make the activity illegal. For example, in 2001, the energy company Enron collapsed after disclosures that the financial statements they were issuing, which were certified by their accountants, Arthur Andersen, LLP, were false and misleading. Thousands of shareholders, including many Enron employees, suffered catastrophic losses through their retirement accounts. These business decisions about accounting methods were not clearly illegal, but they were deemed unethical and state and federal legislatures responded with, among other measures, the Sarbanes-Oxley Act of 2002, also known as the Public Company Accounting Reform and Investor Protection Act. As a result, some of the decisions Enron made, which were ethically question-able, are now also illegal.

Stakeholders to Consider

How can a business generate maximum profits with minimum violations of laws and values? The best advice is for a business to evaluate the effects of its actions on all its *constituents*. This is a tedious process, as the interested parties, or *stakeholders*, include the following:

1. *The shareholders or owners of the business.* The main duty to this group is for the business to make a profit and keep a sterling reputation to encourage new investors.

2. *The employees of the business.* A company has a duty to deal fairly with those who work to make its profit. This includes a duty of loyalty to employees, a duty to provide a safe working environment, and a duty to keep the employees informed of decisions affecting their welfare.

3. *The business partners of the company.* This constituency includes the suppliers, manufacturers, and distributors that the company does busi-ness with on a regular basis. Without ethical treatment to those who the business depends upon to produce and distribute its product, seri-ous problems could result, and problems damage profits.

4. *The customers of the business.* This group buys the product or service the business provides. Customer disapproval is reflected clearly and immediately in sales numbers, which affect profits.

5. *The public at large or the community the business operates in.* This constituency could be very large and only minimally involved in the subject of the business, but a company is a resident of where it does business and has a duty to be a good neighbor.

6. *The environment.* In today's economy, the neighborhood is the planet. Many business decisions affect the environment now and for years to come. Resources are finite; the urge to consume is unlimited. No business can afford to ignore the environmental consequences of its actions in today's world.

If it's legal, is it ethical? If it's ethical, is it legal?

To recap, an ethical decision could be either legal or illegal. For example, Tim may believe it is ethically correct to pay his employees more than minimum wage. That belief was formed from his cultural, religious, and social interactions. Wage and hour laws require only that he pay minimum wage, but he does more. That is a good ethical choice for Tim, and a legal choice. Maybe Sam believes that all employees should earn their wages over a period of time and no employee should start out making more than $1.50 an hour. This could be a strong ethical belief for Sam based on his family traditions and ethnicity. But it would be against the law for Sam to exercise that ethical belief with his employees. Wage and hour laws require employers to pay minimum wage. That is an agreed upon standard in our society, regardless of Sam's personal sense of right and wrong. So an individual's personal ethics could mean that he is more generous or less generous than the law requires.

Could a legal decision be an unethical one? Yes, it could be unethical for you. For example, many people believe it is unethical to use birth control. Their culture, religion, and/or traditions teach that children should be openly welcomed into families. However, the law does not forbid the use of birth control. Every state, which regulates the health and welfare of its citizens, has set forth the conditions under which birth control can be available to it residents. In this instance, some people's personal ethical beliefs make them label this law unethical.

Businesses do not have to do more than the law requires, but because they are living organizations, they have an ethical stance or outlook. If their ethics cause them to fall short of the legal standards, they will face some unpleasant consequences. To avoid violating specific laws, they may find another jurisdiction in which they can do the desired action; for example, they may move the company to cheaper labor centers or to locations with fewer environmental restrictions. However, there are good reasons why businesses may exercise generous ethical standards. These reasons include meeting their stated purpose and being on track with their goals and outlook, but they may also include some less noble or mixed motives, such as the desire for good employee relations, community approval, and better sales.

THE LAW IN ACTION

The decision to move Isabel Bloom, Ltd., to China was not popular. Headlines screamed, "She would be spinning in her grave." (The artist died in 2001.) Endless man-on-the-street interviews quoted collectors saying, "I'll never buy another sculpture." Company officials released statements confirming that it was a very difficult decision and emphasized that workers would be given lengthy notice before the close.

Is the decision a legal one? Absolutely. A business can operate anywhere it wishes. This is a company that ultimately is responsible to its shareholders, and operating more efficiently means bigger profits. Positioning itself to promote nationwide sales also means bigger profits.

Is this decision an ethical one? It depends on what your standards are. If the business applies the principle of utility, its goal is to ensure the greatest good for the greatest number. A utilitarian focus would involve employing more people, making more profits for shareholders, and selling more products. If the business applies the principle of egoism, its goal is to do anything for more take-home dollars for the top people. If the business applies the principle of the categorical imperative, its goal would be to do to the employees and shareholders only those actions that it was willing to universalize.

In the end, why was this decision made? According to the company's statement, management decided to make this move because doing so allowed for production savings and better positioning for the company to distribute its product nationwide. Profit concerns and business issues appear to have trumped historical and community concerns.

When the announcement to move to China was made February 9, 2006, however, the uproar over the decision was astounding. The publicity for the company was very bad. The customer reaction was extremely negative. It turns out that an Isabel Bloom made in China wouldn't be considered an Isabel Bloom at all. Due to this reaction, on February 21, 2006, the company announced the reversal of the decision to move production to China. The company and employees are staying in Davenport, Iowa. However, the company is still exploring overseas options.

TEST YOURSELF

Since this chapter emphasized that ethical decisions are relative, it would not be appropriate to ask questions with definite answers. Rather, I would like to illustrate some choices companies have made about their ethical decisions and ask you to weigh in on their propriety and the principles at work.

1. In 1978, Ben Cohen and Jerry Greenfield started a small ice cream company in Vermont. Ben & Jerry's was committed to doing business in a socially responsible way. One choice the owners made was to cap executive compensation at seven times that of the lowest paid worker in the company. This measure not only established a sense of fair play within the organization, but also helped the company make fair payments to the local dairy farmers they used as suppliers and kept the morale levels of the company high. There was nothing illegal about this compensation scale, although the market would bear a much higher wage for a CEO of a company this size. The compensation rate did not hurt the profits of the business. Which of the three ethical principles mentioned in this chapter is operating in this choice—the principle of utility, the principle of egoism, or the principle of the categorical imperative? Why?

2. In December of 2000, Robert Nardelli became CEO of Home Depot. He ran the company for five years, increasing the revenue and profits

of the business. The share price however, lost ground. Shareholder return over the period was down 13 percent. Since Mr. Nardelli's compensation package was made public in each yearly report, by 2006, it was widely known that he had earned over $200 million in salary and bonuses and was set to keep earning bonuses regardless of the company's performance. Mr. Nardelli resigned in January of 2007. There was nothing illegal about this compensation scale, and in the market, Nardelli could get a similar package elsewhere. The compensation rate did not hurt the profits of the business. Which of the three ethical principles mentioned in this chapter is operating in this choice? Why?

3. In March of 2005, the American College of Physician Executives released results of a survey of physician leaders. When asked about their concerns, 78 percent of those responding indicated they were "very concerned" or "moderately concerned" about physicians overtreating patients to boost income, and 76 percent were "very concerned" or "moderately concerned" about the influence on physicians by pharmaceutical companies. Which of the three ethical principles mentioned in this chapter is operating in these responses? Why?

4. In early 2007, the Attorney General of New York began investigating the relationship between student loan companies and universities. Initial evidence suggested some financial aid administrators at the universities had investments in the student loan companies that they were putting on "preferred lender" lists and recommending to students seeking financial aid. In some cases, the financial aid staff members had sold shares for large profits. One of the universities involved has specific rules in their employment handbook specifying that employees should not directly or indirectly have an interest in a business that is in conflict with the employee's duties with the school. Which of the three ethical principles mentioned in this chapter is operating in this situation with the financial aid employees? Why?

Answers can be found on pages 212–213.

KEY POINTS TO REMEMBER

- Ethics is the study of how people should act. People are influenced in their ethical decisions by their culture, religion, and traditions.

- Ethics does not label any culture, religion, or tradition superior to another; it evaluates how people make the choices they do to act as they do.

- Businesses are engaged in commerce to make a profit. Their ethical choices can affect profit.

- An ethical decision could be an illegal decision; a legal decision could be an unethical decision.

- Ethical decisions are not always based on a belief about right action; they can be motivated by a desire for good publicity, social approval, and increased profit.

How Do Businesses Fit In?

A van or truck owned by a business is involved in a traffic accident resulting in property damage and injuries. It happens every day. Can the business be charged with a crime, such as exceeding the speed limit or failing to stop at a red light? Can a business be sued civilly? What if the vehicle owned by the business was not at fault? Could the business then sue another? In what court and for what recovery? Does the dispute have to go to court, or can a business take advantage of alternative dispute resolution? And finally, is a business governed by the U.S. Constitution, statutes, and case law precedent? Is a business entitled to a speedy trial, the right to free speech, and the protection against self-incrimination?

In this chapter, we will review the introductory chapters as they apply specifically to business rights and responsibilities.

WHAT'S AHEAD

- Businesses and Constitutional Guarantees
- Businesses, Statutory Law, and Common Law
- Businesses and Crimes

- Businesses, Civil Litigation, and ADR
- Businesses in Court
- Businesses and Self-Incrimination

IN THE REAL WORLD

Before November of 2005, Gregg Photography, Inc., was operating a small business in Des Moines, Iowa. The owners were parents Tom and Cindy Gregg and their son, Bob. The business specialized in photography for graduations, anniversaries, new babies, and other events, but its bread and butter was its wedding photography. The business would always have a number of weddings "on the books," meaning it had entered into a contract to photograph the event, provide proofs, and finish photographs. It often received a down payment or upfront money on the services. In November of 2005, numerous complaints were made to the Polk County attorney's office about Gregg Photography, Inc. Ten customers were identified as having problems with Gregg's services; eight of those had filed criminal complaints with the police department. Apparently Gregg was holding over $9,000 of customer deposits for services the customers never received.

Has Gregg Photography, Inc., committed a crime? Can the business be put in jail? Do the dissatisfied customers have any recourse against the company? How can they pursue this? What do they want from Gregg Photography?

KEY CONCEPTS

The court applies the U.S. Constitution, statutes, and common law to businesses just as it does to people. Businesses are therefore liable if they violate public standards of conduct, just like individual citizens—but there are some differences in the way this plays out.

Businesses and Constitutional Guarantees

Language in the commerce clause of the Constitution (article I, section 8) gives the national government the right to regulate commerce in the United States. That means the federal government can pass rules binding a business's dealings with other businesses, customers, and the public. Examples of these regulations include laws regulating interstate transportation, equal employment opportunity, and taxes. In addition, states possess *police powers* and are allowed under the Constitution to pass laws regarding the health, safety, morals, and general welfare of its citizens. That means the state government can pass rules binding a business. Examples of state regulation of business include restaurant health standards, licensing of medical professionals, and workers' compensation laws.

The Constitution also guarantees to a business many of the freedoms recognized for individuals in the Bill of Rights. A company has the ability to exercise free speech. For example, a business could promote one candidate over another for public office or speak out in support of proposed legislation. However, there may be good reason that a business would not exercise this right because taking a stand on an issue may alienate some customers and members of the public. A state may limit a business's commercial speech (advertisements) if there is a valid interest due to health, safety, morals, or general welfare issues. For example, a company can have a really tacky label on its bottle of beer, if it wants that image; it cannot, however, have an obscene label on its product.

Businesses are granted freedom of religion under the Constitution. For a business, this really means freedom from religion, as the government cannot limit the days a business is open. Commerce occurs freely in this country on Saturdays, Sundays, and religious holidays. A business also cannot discriminate on religious grounds in its hiring practices or dealings with customers. For example, a bakery cannot refuse to hire an atheist as an employee or decline to serve a Protestant customer.

Finally, the Constitution guarantees to a business due process of law, which means that government cannot take "life, liberty, or property" from a business without procedures that safeguard fairness. Therefore, a business is protected from unreasonable search and seizure. Federal or state officials cannot come to a business site and demand entry or documents without a search warrant. However, some federal or state representatives could come to a place of business on routine, limited inspections, such as for an Occupational Safety and Health Administration (OSHA) inspection of the premises where worker safety is involved, like the shop floor, but not where other matters are kept, like the basement file room.

Businesses, Statutory Law, and Common Law. A business is also bound by the federal and state statutes that regulate it. Not every statute a legislature passes pertains to a business, so not every rule applies, but a business has to be aware of the rules and regulations required in its industry to keep its operation legal. A business is also bound by the decisions that have been rendered in past federal and state court cases. Precedent applies to a company just as it does to an individual and helps a business predict how its claim or dispute may turn out.

Businesses and Crimes

We can all think of ways in which a business can commit a crime. A local financial firm may *commingle* its money with that of its clients. That is a crime. A large corporation may mislead investors and employees about its financial health with exaggerated profit and loss reports. That is a crime. A sandwich shop could serve tainted food to customers. That is a crime. Or a craft business could have unsafe wiring that causes a customer to sustain a severe electrical shock. That is a crime.

Businesses can commit misdemeanors or felonies. They can pay fines and lose licenses and privileges, but a business cannot be put in jail. If a business commits a felony, for which the consequence could be a prison sentence, the responsible representatives of the business are charged and subject to this penalty. The person charged is the person most directly responsible for the felonious activity—usually an officer or director of the company if the crime relates to a business decision, or the employee involved if the crime relates to an accident or injury. A business charged with a crime cannot be subject to double jeopardy and enjoys the right to a speedy criminal trial, the right to have assistance of counsel, and the right to confront the witnesses against them.

A business could also be the victim of a crime, such as robbery, employee *embezzlement*, or purchase of supplies that are never received. The public prosecutor represents business victims as well as individual victims of crime. Again, a company representative would be making the complaint on behalf of the business. If the accused is found guilty of the crime, any fine is paid into the public coffers. The purpose of a business's pursuing a criminal complaint is to uphold the standards set by society and keep the public safe from a recurrence of this type of event.

Businesses, Civil Litigation, and ADR

A business may be liable to another for a civil matter—based either on a breach of contract or a tort. If accused of violating a personal standard of conduct to another, a business has to hire legal representation and defend itself. If the business is found liable, it may be ordered to pay damages to the injured party. A side effect of being involved in a legal claim could be bad publicity and lost goodwill. Because the publicity could be as detrimental as the claim itself, businesses favor the use of alternative dispute resolution, such as negotiation, mediation, and arbitration. ADR is cheaper, faster, and much less public than a civil trial. A business may sue others for civil damages. To do so, it must hire legal representation and pursue the matter. The business goes through the same processes as an individual claimant to try to recover damages.

Businesses in Court

Businesses may resolve disputes in federal court if they qualify—that is, if the matter involved is about a federal question or if there is diversity jurisdiction. To qualify for federal diversity jurisdiction, the plaintiff and the defendant in the lawsuit have to be from different states. But in what state does a business reside? Federal rules state that a business resides in every state where it does business. Businesses may also avail themselves of state courts to resolve any disputes. They have access to court in any state in which they do business. Like every other criminal defendant, a business is presumed innocent until proven guilty of a criminal charge beyond a reasonable doubt. Like every other civil defendant, a business needs to prove its case by a preponderance of the evidence.

Businesses and Self-Incrimination. There is one significant limitation on a business in a criminal situation. The Fifth Amendment to the Constitution provides that no person in a criminal case "shall be compelled…to be a witness against himself." This right guarantees that a person charged with a crime has no obligation to provide personal incriminating records to prosecutors, although prosecutors may try to obtain relevant written records by discovery. This right also guarantees that an accused can refuse to testify on his own behalf in a criminal matter and that this failure to testify cannot be construed against the accused. This is not the case for a business. A business cannot refuse to provide business records, even if they contain incriminating information against the business or an employee, officer, or contact of the business. The Fifth Amendment protection is for persons, not for businesses. Likewise, a business cannot testify in a criminal matter. It would be unwieldy to put Ford Motor Company on the witness stand. A business appears in court through its representatives, mainly individuals who are officers or directors of the company. Those individuals cannot claim the Fifth Amendment and refuse to testify because what they say may be incriminating to the business entity. Those individuals could assert the Fifth Amendment for themselves; however, if any of the questions would elicit information, that may incriminate the witnesses personally.

THE LAW IN ACTION

According to the Iowa Code, depriving another of his property is theft. The crime of theft is classified according to degrees, depending on the seriousness of the theft.

The amount of money Gregg Photography, Inc., held for its complaining customers fell into the category of second-degree theft, which is punishable by a fine of between $5,000 and $7,000 and a prison sentence of up to five years. Taking another's money at this level is a felony.

The Polk County attorney charged Gregg Photography, Inc., with one *count* (charge) of theft. The Greggs voluntarily talked to the police and the prosecutor, explaining that Tom and Cindy were really not part of the business; they had only agreed to give Bob some money to start up his business and in return got some shares of stock in the corporation. Bob was the one who ran the business day to day and did all the photography. Apparently things had gotten tight, with the rent on the location, the unexpected expense of some new equipment, and a slow fall season. Bob was doing the best he could, but he fell behind in jobs and missed some other jobs completely. He was ignoring the calls from angry customers but never meant for anyone to be harmed. Despite all the causes of the difficulty, Gregg Photography, Inc., had committed theft. It had deprived others of their property. The business could be tried on the charge and could be liable to pay a significant fine.

Because this offense was a felony, and the possibility of jail time was also an issue, the Polk County attorney had to make a decision as to what business owners or officers should be charged with the crime. Obviously, the business itself cannot go to prison. In this case, the county attorney determined that Bob was the managing owner and the one who should have prevented the situation. Since they were all owners of a small business, Tom and Cindy could also be charged with breaking this law, but the county attorney used his discretion and did not charge them. If Bob and Gregg Photography, Inc., were found guilty beyond a reasonable doubt of committing theft, the company would be liable for a big fine and probably also lose its license to operate within the city of Des Moines. For a small business already in financial difficulty, a guilty verdict would mean the end—of money, of authority to operate, of customers, of goodwill. For Bob, a guilty verdict would mean a big monetary debt and prison time.

In preparation for the criminal trial of *State v. Gregg Photography, Inc.,* the defendants would be able to confront the complaining customers and have counsel represent them (although not a public defender, because they are not indigent). The state would have the right to subpoena business records showing the contracts and deposits received. Bob Gregg could not object to providing these business records because they are the business's property, not his personally, and a business has no Fifth Amendment right against self-incrimination. The defendants would also be entitled to a speedy trial and the presumption of innocence until proven guilty beyond a reasonable doubt. To prove the case, the county attorney would call the customers as witnesses, show the business records of the deposits received, and refer to the Iowa statute that defines the offense.

In this case, the Polk County attorney worked out a resolution with Gregg Photography and Bob Gregg before a trial was ever necessary. The defendants were remorseful that this happened. The parents stepped forward and agreed to pay any deficient amounts. Bob agreed to plead guilty to a less serious degree of theft and pay a fine. The business lost its license to operate in Des Moines. If Bob ever tried to get a business license in Iowa in the future, the theft conviction would prevent him from doing so. Justice was served. The resolution recognized the crime, the defendants paid a fine, and the public was protected from this happening again.

The Greggs were not completely off the hook, though. There were still angry customers. Although the parents had resources to return all down payments, some customers still felt they had a cause of action against the business for products that were never received. Some customers demanded the services they already contracted for, since wedding photographers are hard to find on short notice. Some customers could not be appeased with a returned deposit because their events had not been photographed at all. In cases where Bob missed jobs, there were no photos taken to process. Any and all of these customers could sue Gregg Photography, Inc., in state court for breach of contract and the damages that resulted from the breach. Instead, all the claims were mediated to conclusion. Some claims were resolved with the return of the deposit, some with the delivery of photo albums, and some with significant additional compensation to parties without a wedding album, since precious memories lost are hard to value.

Since this incident caused bad publicity generally for photographers in the area, a number of colleagues of Gregg Photography, Inc., stepped up and offered to finish developing photos or retake photos for injured customers at no cost. This helped a fellow photographer meet his obligations and softened the bad press all photographers were suffering.

TEST YOURSELF

1. Davis County wanted to increase the local sales tax by 1 percent to provide more revenue for county roads and infrastructure repairs. The local chamber of commerce was against this measure due to the already high sales taxes that county residents paid. Many businesses in town contributed to the chamber of commerce to support their campaign to defeat this initiative on the March ballot. Can a business make such a contribution legally?

2. In the year 2000, it was disclosed that the federal government had been investigating the Royal Caribbean Cruise Lines for environmental violations. Evidence showed that the company had used tactics such as hidden piping and night dumping to discharge thousands of gallons of waste products, including oily bilge, photo-developing chemicals, and dry-cleaner fluids. Affected waterways included the New York harbor, the Port of Miami, and the Alaskan Inside Passage. What legal consequences could Royal Caribbean face if these claims are proven?

3. Mr. Paul Max has run Max Tax Service, Inc., for six years. Although the business is incorporated, he is the only owner of shares and makes all the management decisions. Max Tax Service, Inc., is being audited by the Internal Revenue Service regarding its corporate tax liability for the year 2005. The IRS has subpoenaed some corporate tax records, but Mr. Max does not wish to provide them. He is *pleading the Fifth*, which means he is invoking his right not to incriminate himself accorded to him by the Fifth Amendment of the Constitution. Will he be successful?

Brain Teaser

4. In a 2002 advertising campaign, Nike, Inc., claimed that it protected rights of laborers in overseas factories that made its footwear. A labor activist, Marc Kasky, did not believe this was a valid claim and sued the corporation in the state of California for false advertising. Nike defended the suit saying that it was protected by the First Amendment right to freedom of speech. Who should win this dispute and why?

Answers can be found on pages 213–214.

KEY POINTS TO REMEMBER

- A business entity can commit a crime or have a crime committed against it.

- A business entity can commit a civil violation or have a civil violation committed against it.

- The Constitution of the United States grants some rights to businesses just as it does to individuals, but a business does not enjoy all the protections granted to individual citizens.

- A business can sue and be sued in federal and state courts depending on where it does business.

- A business can use alternative dispute resolution to resolve claims.

II

CIVIL LAW IN DETAIL

Now that we have some background information about the law, the process of litigation, and alternative dispute resolution, we are ready to examine civil law in more detail. Part II outlines how to determine liability for a tort or for a breach of contract. In addition, this section provides defenses to such claims so that a business faced with these actions might know how to establish rightful claims and respond to wrongful ones.

The Recipe for a Tort

When I got married, I was a 25-year-old law school graduate with what I thought was a certain level of sophistication. I don't know why it hit me with such shock when I realized that my student specialties of ham sandwiches and cheap spaghetti would not create the kind of homey, romantic dinner hour I longed for. Julia Child to the rescue. In no time, I was offering my mate Chicken Supreme and Boeuf Bourguignon. I swear if I had learned to make the Eminence Brune—a bittersweet, dense chocolate cake—earlier, he would have proposed two years before.

This chapter is not about tortes, the dessert, but it is about recipes. The law is a lot like cooking. If you have all the necessary ingredients, you can create the desired product. Cooking up a civil tort claim is a matter of having all the right elements fall into place, and in this chapter we'll put together an easy-to-follow, foolproof recipe.

IN THE REAL WORLD

In 1999, a tragic accident occurred near Janesville, Wisconsin, involving a van filled with high school and college students working to sell magazine subscriptions on their Easter break. Youth Employment Services, LLC, and its related company, Subscriptions Plus, Inc., operated out of Iowa and Oklahoma, respectively. They hired 20-year-old Jeremy Holmes to work as a driver and handler for groups traveling to various communities to sell subscriptions door-to-door. On the evening of March 25, a Milton Township police officer clocked a van on I-90 going about 80 miles per hour. He pulled onto the interstate to follow and saw the vehicle veer off the road, begin to roll, and throw about 12 people onto the highway. Fourteen people were in the van; seven were killed and five were seriously injured.

Is what happened a tragic accident? An act of God? A crime? A tort?

KEY CONCEPTS

A tort is a personal injury. The law allows a person who is injured by the actions of another to recover from that person if all the right elements are in place. Tort law is a branch of civil law, which concerns the rights of individuals to recover against one another. The usual method of recovery is to sue for damages. One action can result in both a crime and a tort claim because one action can violate a public and a private standard of conduct.

Types of Torts

If my neighbor misses a stoplight and runs his car into my lovely 1998 Honda Accord, this could be a crime and it could also be a tort. To determine whether it is a crime, the law will look at the facts and his *state of mind*. Did he mean to do it? If so, it was an *intentional* act and is considered a serious offense. Society does not approve of people intentionally breaking a law. Was he driving too fast for conditions? If so, he was probably reckless. *Reckless* is the description used in the law for behavior about which you should have known better. My neighbor should have known better than to drive his car considering that he knew the brakes were getting funny. Or, he should have known better than to talk on the phone while driving. Being reckless is troubling behavior; the law usually doesn't ignore this type of action, but it doesn't consider it as diabolical as intentional misconduct. Maybe he was just negligent. *Negligent* is the description used in the law for behavior that is careless. He didn't mean to cause an accident. He had no warning that something might happen, but he wasn't being as careful as he should have been. *Negligence* describes a true accident, unintended and unforeseen, but damaging nevertheless. Negligence is very common and usually not as serious in its consequences as recklessness or intentional acts.

To determine how to classify the seriousness of a tort, you use the terms intentional, reckless, and negligent, which are the same words used to classify crimes. The more serious and purposeful the injury, the more serious the damages. Certainly if my neighbor intends to run a stop sign and hit my car, I should recover damages from him. If he intended me no harm, but should have known better than to drive after taking that antihistamine tablet, he should be responsible for the damages he probably could have kept from happening. My neighbor's conduct was reckless. But under what conditions could he be found negligent? Should he only have to fix my 1998 Honda or should he have to buy me a Lexus? If he intended to harm me, the deliberate collision probably caused more damage than a reckless or negligent act would have caused. When is something just a dumb accident and when is it a legitimate legal claim?

Ingredients for a Tort of Negligence

To establish negligence, the law requires certain ingredients to be present. These include duty, breach, damage, and causation. Since civil law gives a place for people to recover for personal breaches of conduct, negligence involves a breach of a rule of conduct, or a *duty*. To weigh the duty involved, the law creates the *reasonable person* by asking, "What would a reasonable person do in these circumstances?" Would a reasonable person believe there was a duty? Would a reasonable person think she should be able to drive to the corner store for a quart of milk without getting plowed into at a stoplight? Of course she would. Laws and regulations imply that members of society have duties to one another. We have traffic laws and regulations on who can drive. Drivers have a duty to other drivers. Employers have a duty to their employees to provide a safe workplace. A teacher has a duty to the students to keep tabs on them during school hours, not just drop them off at the mall on a whim for a field trip. A parent has a duty to a child. A business has a duty to its customers invited into its parking lot and store location.

The mythical reasonable person cannot be an overly sensitive type. For example, someone who never uses coarse language cannot sue you because you utter a "darn" within earshot. Having a duty to be reasonable in public situations doesn't mean you have to be a prude. On the other hand, if you think Howard Stern is a brilliant conversationalist, you may run into problems in dealing with others. You can usually figure out what is acceptable and reasonable behavior in most circumstances.

If my neighbor had a duty to me at the intersection, he cannot be liable to me unless he breaches that duty. To *breach* your duty is to break it or violate it by not being reasonable. He breaches his duty to me if he runs into my car. A toy manufacturer breaches its duty to its customers if it distributes baby toys that have removable parts that can choke infants. A business breaches its duty to its shareholders if it falsifies financial statements to encourage investors.

The third ingredient necessary for a tort claim is *damage*. To be considered a tort, an action must cause some injury either to a person or to property. If no injury results from your breach of duty, you do not have a tort claim. Hurt pride will not do it. Broken bones and medical bills will. Some injury lawsuits ask for *pain and suffering* or emotional distress damages. These are generally hard for the law to value and are likely to result in *money damages* only if they go along with real physical injuries or damaged property.

Finally, tort law requires the liable party to be a cause of the hurt. My neighbor's actions have to directly contribute to the injury that results. This is where many tort claims fail in part or in total. As a society, we are quick to blame others when things go wrong. For example, he did run that stoplight, but the city hung the light in an awkward spot on that corner, and he couldn't see it clearly. Or, he did run that stoplight, but he just had his car serviced and the mechanic must have damaged the brakes. Or, he did run that stoplight, but he was late for work and would lose his job if he didn't get there on time, so it was his boss's fault. *Causation* is also hard to prove on occasion because injuries result from more than one cause. For example, my neighbor did run that stoplight, but I was not watching the intersection as closely as I should have been before proceeding.

So there you have it, the recipe for a tort. To hold the person committing a tort—called a *tortfeasor*—liable for his action, you have to prove duty, breach, damage, and causation. If you don't have all four, you don't have a tort. What do you have?

Well, you could have an accident, such as knocking a person's books out of her hands in a crowded hallway. In a crowded hallway, it is reasonable that this may happen, and if there are no real damages, you don't take that matter to court. You could have a freak accident, like the weekend warrior who was working on an important project in the garage, climbed up on the table saw to reach a shelf, and lost his balance. The leg gash was pretty bad; it could have been much worse. Did the company making the saw have a duty to warn users not to use the tool as a ladder? Would a reasonable person have expected someone to use the tool as a ladder? Sure, terrible damage resulted, but some of the elements of a tort aren't present—there wasn't a clear duty here, and the cause of the incident was not the direct fault of the manufacturer.

For over 16 years, ABC has presented "almost torts" on their show *America's Funniest Home Videos*. This program catalogs one potential tortfeasor after another, where victims suffer a social blunder often involving a wedding, some food disaster, or a spontaneous foul-up. Often animal antics are involved. These fall short of torts, because they generally don't highlight injuries other than damaged pride, and the property damage is minimal though essential to the slapstick quality.

Damages in Tort Cases

If you do have a winning recipe and all the ingredients of a tort claim are present, you recover damages. That is, you are compensated for your loss. On occasion, damages include more than just the immediate losses that occur. I may need a rental car for two days while the Honda is being fixed, and the only reason I need it is because my neighbor damaged my car, so he should also pay for the rental car. This type of additional damage is called *incidental* (because it goes along with the original tort) or *consequential* (because it is a result of the original tort), so the tortfeasor is liable. If I am hurt in the accident with my neighbor, my damages may include payment of costs for medical treatment and recovery, including hospital bills, physical therapy costs, and lost wages while I am off work. Generally these amounts are supposed to put me back in the position I would have been in if the accident had not occurred; they are not to unjustly enrich the victim.

The rare tort claim results in punitive damages being awarded to the victim. Punitive damages are over and above any compensatory damages and are meant to punish the tortfeasor for his actions. One of the most famous punitive damages cases is the McDonald's coffee case. In this case, a 79-year-old lady sued McDonald's for damages because of third-degree burns she suffered when a Styrofoam cup of coffee purchased through a drive-up window spilled in her lap. A jury awarded her $200,000 in damages and $2.7 million in punitive damages.

McDonald's was punished for this accident because it was brought to the jury's attention that the restaurant had had more than 700 burn claims over 10 years because of its scalding-hot coffee. McDonald's kept its coffee at a temperature significantly hotter than any other restaurant's to protect the flavor, it claimed, but also to save the product longer before having to throw it away. This knowledge of the danger of the product, coupled with the profit motive involved, probably persuaded the jury that this was not a case of negligence but rather a case of reckless, *willful* behavior on the part of the tortfeasor to value profit over safety. The award of $2.7 million is a staggeringly large amount; it is also the profit McDonald's made on two days' worth of coffee sales. Sometimes, civil courts allow for punitive damages to motivate a tortfeasor to make some significant changes in the way he does business. Immediately after this case, the temperature of McDonald's coffee dropped from 190 degrees to 155 degrees.

After similar punitive damages awards, tobacco companies got serious about their warning programs and changed their marketing techniques, and Ford and Firestone recalled the tires on the Explorer that were prone to explode.

Defenses to Claims of Negligence

It is hard to defend yourself if you commit an intentional tort. In some instances, you can argue self-defense or defense of others if your actions harm a person. Recklessness, by its very definition, means you should have known better than to do your action, so it is difficult to defend yourself in this case, because it presumes a certain callousness or willfulness in the face of better judgment. However, there are some defenses that a person accused of committing a negligent tort may use to shield herself from liability. They include the following:

1. *Consent.* In some cases, the injured party knows that a possibility of harm may result from the action taken. Bungee jumping off a bridge or cliff is fraught with danger. That is part of its appeal. Things can go wrong, and if they do, the result is usually serious. Therefore, the service provider may require the customer to sign a consent form or a waiver of liability, recognizing the fact that the customer agrees to hold the service provider harmless from any damage that may occur.

    Businesses use consents and waivers all the time. Every time you park in a parking garage, there is a waiver form on your ticket stub. The owner of the garage is not liable for any damage that may occur to your car while it is parked there. Every car wash is enter-at-your-own-risk. Sometimes customers are asked to sign what I call preemptive consents. Your bank has disclosed the overdraft fees in their original agreement, which you signed, so you can't complain about them now.

2. *Contributory or comparative negligence.* This is the classic defense to a tort claim. When a tortfeasor argues contributory negligence, she is saying that even if she committed a tort, she should not be liable because someone else contributed to the harm caused. The usual contributor is the victim himself.

    My neighbor should have stopped at the red light but since I was not driving as safely as I should have been, my neighbor is off the hook. He could not be the cause of the harm because I was in the wrong, too. *Contributory negligence* is a harsh rule. If verified, it usually bars the victim from recovery. Few victims are blameless. Few accidents have one cause only; they often are a collaborative effort. So today, most states have abandoned the contributory negligence doctrine for the rule of comparative negligence. With *comparative negligence*, a judge or jury can weigh the causation of an accident and apportion the blame among the parties, ordering each to pay his fair share of the damages. In my car accident, perhaps my neighbor is 80 percent to blame and I am 20 percent responsible. If my losses were $100, he would have to pay $80 and I would have to absorb the rest of my loss.

    Comparative negligence is really about determining the causation ingredient of a tort by considering all the parties that may cause a tort. There is a time limit to causation. In a personal injury case, it is usually a year and a day. If the victim doesn't die within that time, the tortfeasor is probably not liable for causing the victim's death, whenever it does occur. Intervening and superseding causes can diminish a tortfeasor's liability also. For example, if the ambulance taking me to the hospital for stitches after my collision with my neighbor is involved in a serious accident, my neighbor is probably not held responsible for my broken neck.

3. *Assumption of the risk.* This is related to consent and to contributory negligence. With *assumption of the risk*, the tortfeasor argues that the victim assumed some responsibility for what happened. If you engage in extreme fighting, you could get hurt; if you go hunting, you could be the victim of an accident; if you choose to exit a burning building via the elevator, you could get injured severely.

Strict Liability

There are a few instances in which the law recognizes liability for a tort even if all the elements are not present. This liability without negligence is called *strict liability*.

The law takes this unusual step because certain situations are impossible to make safe and when they cause harm, the injury is usually quite severe. Therefore the law imposes an absolute duty that the victim be compensated by the person causing the harm. Strict liability generally applies to those who deal in an ultrahazardous business or with defective products. Examples of ultrahazardous businesses are chemical companies, rock quarries, and manufacturers that produce toxic waste. Examples of defective products can be found in chapter 11.

THE LAW IN ACTION

The accident outside of Janesville, Wisconsin, was a tragedy. It also resulted in criminal charges against the driver, the company that employed him, and the owners of the company. In addition, child labor law violations were filed against the companies in Oklahoma and Wisconsin, but we want to analyze the facts to see if any tort liability is present.

That evening 14 youngsters, aged 15 to 25 years, were riding in the van driven by Jeremy Holmes. The van had adequate seat belts, but none of the passengers were wearing one. After Jeremy sped past the police car, he tried to switch seats with another passenger to change drivers, and in that maneuver, the van rolled and left the highway. Jeremy did not have a valid Wisconsin driver's license at the time of the accident. The van was unregistered and unlicensed, but was insured for personal use by the owner of Youth Employment Services, LLC. That owner, Choan Alan Lane, knew that Jeremy had been arrested for previous traffic offenses and had no valid license. The owner of the company also knew that Jeremy used marijuana frequently, mainly because they smoked it together.

To establish a claim for tort damages, a plaintiff must prove duty, breach, damages, and causation. In this case, each injured person wished to bring a tort claim against the driver, the company that was their employer, and the owner of the company.

The first ingredient necessary to prove a tort based on negligence is duty. The employer, Youth Employment Services, LLC, had a duty to provide a safe working environment for its employees. One issue in this case was that the company argued that the youth were not employees of the company, but rather independent contractors selling on commission. This point is irrelevant in the analysis of duty, as even an independent contractor forced to ride in the principal's vehicle should expect safe transport. The driver, Jeremy Holmes, had a duty to care for his crew safely. He breached that duty by driving 80 miles per hour in an unregistered, unlicensed vehicle without valid authority to drive. The owner of the company, Choan Alan Lane, had a duty to act responsibly as a company owner and officer. He did not do so in that he falsified records about the van's use, knew the vehicle was unlicensed and unregistered, and knew Jeremy Holmes was unfit to drive and lead a crew. All three potential defendants had a duty to each victim.

Did the defendants' actions establish the second element of a tort claim—that is, a breach of duty? Yes, in each case, because each defendant was careless, if not reckless, to allow this chain of events to go forward.

The third element in a tort claim is damages. Did the breach of duty cause damages? Tragically, seven youth were killed and five were seriously injured. In the case of a deceased victim, his or her representative usually sues the tortfeasor for wrongful death. A judgment finding the tortfeasor liable for wrongful death would order him to pay damages. The term *guilty* is not used in civil cases; the defendant is found to be either liable or not liable. Damages for a lost life would depend on the age of the victim, his economic prospects had he survived, and the consequential and incidental expenses due to the death, such as expenses to dependants and loved ones who no longer have the services and affection of the victim.

One of the crash victims suffered severe brain damage. His damages include future medical expenses and treatment costs, lost income potential, and special living arrangements necessary for the rest of his life. One 15-year-old girl was paralyzed from the waist down and has minimal use of her arms and fingers. Her paralysis has led to many complications including lung problems and bladder infections. In one year her bills at one hospital exceeded $200,000. The girl's mother worked as a lab technician, but she had to give up the job to provide round-the-clock care for her daughter. Clearly, these two victims have substantial and ongoing damages from this incident.

The final element in a tort claim is causation. Did the defendants' actions cause the damages that occurred? Are there any defenses that would protect the defendants from liability? It is true that all the victims signed up to work for this traveling magazine sales company. They knew traveling in a van was part of the job, but this knowledge is not consent to be involved in a highway accident. They also did not use the seat belts available in the vehicle. Failure to use seat belts is a contributing factor to the victims' injuries, but by far the biggest cause of this tragedy was the negligence of the driver and the company employing him. Could the tortfeasors claim that the real cause of the accident was the police officer by the side of the road who clocked the van, scared the unlicensed driver, and precipitated the accident? No, the police officer had every right to be there, and a reasonable person would know that. A reasonable person would not have driven with the record that Jeremy Holmes had. A reasonable employer would not have allowed such an employee to supervise a sales crew and drive a van. A reasonable company owner would not have put into commercial use a van that was unlicensed, unregistered, and improperly insured.

This event satisfies all the requirements of a tort of gross negligence with grave damages. Gross negligence is most serious because it is a conscious, voluntary act that amounts to a reckless disregard of a legal duty. You cannot say that any of the tortfeasors intended to harm the victims, but by their utter indifference to the welfare of others, they came very close to intentional behavior. The victims did receive some compensation for their damages from insurance that was available, but not enough to meet their future needs or compensate for the losses.

Exact figures on the damages victims recovered are unavailable because of settled claims and sealed court records. The tortfeasors were wiped out financially, and they have also faced felony criminal charges stemming from this incident.

TEST YOURSELF

As a tribute to television past and present, I'd like to take the exercise examples from classical moments on the small screen.

1. In the opening credits to *The Dick Van Dyke Show*, a jolly Rob Petrie comes home to New Rochelle, New York, after a busy day writing comedy. He kisses his wife, Laura. He walks into the living room and takes a classic pratfall over the ottoman, arms and legs flailing. He bounces one last time onto his feet, smiling and happy. Tort or no tort?

2. In a 1991 episode of *L.A. Law*, the senior partner, Leland McKenzie, is speaking with a fellow attorney and former paramour, Rosalind Shays, as they leave the office. They are getting heated in their remarks. The elevator door opens, Rosalind walks into the elevator with one last zinger to Leland, and—*Ahhhh!*— the audience hears a fading scream and a splat. The elevator was not functioning properly. The episode was titled "Good to the Last Drop." Tort or no tort?

3. In a 2005 episode of *Las Vegas*, new casino owner Monica Mancuso is on the roof arguing with Danny McCoy. She is dressed in a wild, kimono-sleeved gown. A huge gust of wind comes along and flies her off the roof while Styx's "Come Sail Away" is playing for the fade-out. We learn in the next episode that she lands in the front window of a high-end shoe store. Tort or no tort?

4. CBS had next year's ratings in the bag when they ended the 1979–80 season of *Dallas* with the mother of all cliff-hangers. Who shot JR? Tort or no tort?

Answers can be found on pages 214–215.

KEY POINTS TO REMEMBER

- A tort is a personal injury for which the law gives a remedy, usually damages, to put the injured party back in the position he was in before the incident happened.

- Torts, like crimes, can be caused by intentional, reckless, or negligent conduct.

- The more serious the intention to cause harm, the more serious the consequences; the more serious the harm caused, the more serious the consequences.

- To recover for a tort, you need to have all these ingredients: duty, breach, damages, and causation.

- If the recipe falls short of an ingredient, you do not have a tort. You may have an embarrassment, or a blunder, or a really good entry for *America's Funniest Home Videos*.

- If you have a winning recipe, you can recover for your losses and some related expenses. In rare instances, tort claims can result in punitive damages.

- To protect yourself against a tort claim, you may be able to use defenses to offset liability. Defenses include consent, assumption of the risk, and contributory and comparative negligence.

- On occasion, the law doesn't care if you have the recipe exactly right to establish a tort. It imposes strict liability on individuals who engage in unusually dangerous activity.

The Recipe for a Contract

Today is a typical Thursday. It is 10:45 in the morning, and I have already entered into or exercised my rights in at least 10 contracts.

I went out to my car at about 7:10 A.M. to drive my husband to his job. I was confident doing so because I know I have adequate car insurance in force to protect me, my car, and my sleepy husband.

We stopped at the bagel shop. I contracted for a plain bagel and a coffee. On the way out, I purchased a newspaper from the stand on the corner.

I dropped my husband off at work, because he has a contract to be there by 8:00 A.M., and I headed home. Before I could begin work, I needed to check the news, and thanks to an agreement with the local cable provider, I am able to do that by switching on the television.

Finally, it is time to get to work, so I fire up the new laptop, still under warranty, and do some online research thanks to my contract with the Internet provider.

At about 10:00, I go to the refrigerator for some orange juice that I purchased at the local grocer yesterday. I get a call from the water company about coming to read the inside meter at a time when I am home. We have a contract that provides for periodic, inside checks. With all this contracting going on, it is a wonder there is any time to write, and this chapter is due, by contract, before the end of this month!

There is nothing to be intimidated about when you consider studying contracts. You have been using them every day, all day, for years. This chapter will put that knowledge into focus.

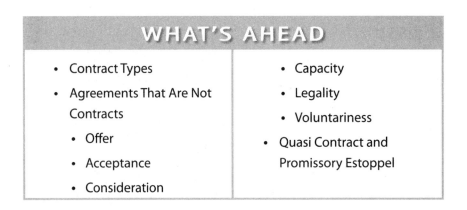

WHAT'S AHEAD

- Contract Types
- Agreements That Are Not Contracts
  - Offer
  - Acceptance
  - Consideration
- Capacity
- Legality
- Voluntariness
- Quasi Contract and Promissory Estoppel

IN THE REAL WORLD

Mr. and Mrs. Buyer were thrilled to be looking for their first house. They had a list of everything they wanted: an older home, a yard for the kids, and hardwood floors. They had this image of their family lounging in the living room—fire in the fireplace, Christmas tree in the corner, and gleaming oak beneath their feet. When they saw Mr. and Mrs. Seller's 1920s brick home at 123 Cherry Lane, they were interested. At a second viewing, the Sellers were present and Mrs. Buyer asked Mr. Seller if they had refinished the gorgeous living room and dining room floors themselves. He said they had and, in fact, extra finishing product was still in the basement. Upstairs in the nursery, Mrs. Buyer admired the pine floor, albeit soft wood, and asked Mrs. Seller if all the wood floors in the house were in as good a condition as that floor. Mrs. Seller assured the Buyers that they were. After a third viewing with Mrs. Buyer's parents in tow, an offer was made for $91,000. The asking price was $95,000. After a little wavering, the Sellers accepted the offer by signing the Realtor's form. The house had been for sale for four months and the Sellers were willing to accept this price because they had made an offer on a new home themselves and were set to move shortly.

The closing was to occur four weeks hence, but within one week, the Buyers were so anxious and excited that they called the Sellers to see if they could come over to measure for drapes. No convenient time could be found. About 10 days before the closing, the Buyers tried to arrange a time to review the upstairs layout, but again, the Sellers were just too busy. It was hard to wait, but the Buyers did, until the night before the closing. The Sellers had moved out that day and the Buyers did not see the harm in driving over to look around. They walked up the front steps, stepped onto the big front porch, and lovingly looked through the picture windows into the living room. What? Could it be? They peered in again, and confirmed that the middle of the 15′ × 20′ living room was not gleaming hardwood, but raw plywood. Only about two feet of the room's edges were oak flooring. The Sellers had had a large area rug in this room. The Realtor's description of the floors throughout the house read SOME HARD-WOOD FLOORS.

Did the Buyers and Sellers have a good contract? Did it contain all the necessary ingredients to be enforceable? What if the Buyers did not go through with their agreement? Could the Sellers sue them for damages? What would those damages be?

Do the Buyers have any recourse under the circumstances to defend themselves against a claim that they breached their promise to buy the house?

KEY CONCEPTS

Contract actions, along with torts, make up the two main categories of civil law. In the last chapter, we reviewed torts, or personal injuries, that often arise from an unexpected and unanticipated event. Contracts, on the other hand, are usually willful agreements that people enter into, but they come in many shapes and sizes. It is easy to get intimidated with all the specialized contract terms that legal and business texts throw around, but many of these terms make perfect sense if you think about them with examples.

Contract Types

Contracts can be written, like a lease agreement for your apartment, or they can be oral, like going into a paint store and getting a gallon of Contemplation Green. Some people get all excited about this point and think a valid contract must be written down, but that is not true in most cases. By far, the majority of contracts people enter into are oral.

Contracts may be express or implied. If they are expressed, they have been expressed orally or in writing. If they are implied, no words of contracting have been spoken. For example, the paperboy delivers the *Daily Times* to my front door at about 5:00 A.M. He does not knock on the door every day and wake me to ask if I want the paper; he just throws it very hard against the front door. I go to a grocery checkout counter, hold up my candy bar, deposit 50 cents on the counter, and walk out. I don't want a witnessed, written record of that transaction; I don't even have to utter a word because my actions say it all.

Contracts can be executed or executory. These terms refer to the time it takes to complete the agreement. My candy bar purchase is an executed contract. The deal is done, fully performed when I give money and get the chocolate bar. My apartment lease is an executory contract. It is going to be performed over a period of time. It is still ongoing, although the terms have been set and won't change during the length of the lease. I am buying my car with an executory contract. I did not pay for it all at once, but I will be paying over the next 36 months.

Finally, contracts can be valid, void, voidable, or invalid. These terms just describe how binding the agreement is. A *valid* contract is another name for an enforceable contract. A *void* contract might look like it fits the recipe, but it is not enforceable because of a term or condition. A *voidable* contract does fit the recipe, but the law may still refuse to enforce it for some reason. And an *invalid* contract is the same as an unenforceable contract; it does not have all the ingredients necessary to be enforceable.

Agreements That Are Not Contracts

We make a lot of agreements that the law will not enforce, and those should be distinguished from contracts. For example, I tell my son that I will take him to the zoo if he cleans his room. He cannot sue me in a court of law if I fail to get him to the zoo that day. I was just giving him some motivation. I may tell my sister that I will go with her to visit Aunt Peggy. If I have to work that day and do not make the trip, my sister cannot sue me. I just thought it would be a nice gesture to accompany her. If my neighbor drops a bag of groceries unloading her car and I see she has spilled a quart of milk, I may run over and give her the extra quart I have in my refrigerator. I can't sue her if she doesn't reimburse me; I was offering a gift. Other types of agreements that the law will not enforce include ethical obligations ("Our policy is no refunds without a receipt, but you are a regular customer") and sales pitches ("This will be the last dust mop you ever have to buy").

The Recipe for a Contract

Contracts are all about bargains, sales, deals, and agreements. The law will enforce the ones that follow the recipe by having an offer, an acceptance, consideration, capacity, legality, and voluntariness.

Offer. The first element or ingredient is an *offer*. Sometimes people are just talking out a possible scenario: "I might sell my car"; "I'm thinking about a new high definition television"; or "Can't you just see yourself in this sports car?" These preliminary discussions and sales pitches are not offers. Offers must be definite and they must come from a person who has an intention to be bound. Newspaper advertisements are not offers; they are too general and not made to specific individuals. That is why the store can get away with not having the advertised "deal" when you get there.

So someone has to start the ball rolling, and this is the *offeror*. The offeror makes a promise to do something, buy something, exchange something, etc. An example of a specific offer would be "I'll give you $20 for your algebra book." It could also be a nonverbal offer, such as unloading your grocery cart contents on the checkout lane at the supermarket and nodding your head that you found everything you needed. Whether you put it into words or not, your behavior indicates you are offering to purchase those items.

An offer has to be received to be effective, so the offeror must be specific and communicate it to the *offeree*. I cannot step into another person's negotiation and expect the same deal. For example, my brother gets a great credit card offer from American Express but is not interested. I cannot send in the form and accept the offer. The offer was to my brother, not to me. An offer is good for as long as the offeror says it is. The offeror controls this term. If the offeror does not specify how long the offer is good for, it is good for a reasonable time. A reasonable time to respond to buying a load of bananas can be a much shorter time than a reasonable time to respond to an offer to purchase a house. What is reasonable depends on the subject of the contract. If timing is very important, the offeror can specify "Estimate good for 30 days" or whatever other timing he requires.

Acceptance. Once an offer has been communicated by the offeror to the offeree, there are some choices. The offeree may agree to the terms. This is an *acceptance.* The acceptance must be in the same form as the offer. You cannot make any changes, so if the offer is "I will sell you my car for $1,000," the acceptance must be something like "okay" or "deal" or "$1,000 it is." The acceptance cannot be "Okay, $1,000 for your car and an extra set of tires." This requirement that the offeree accept exactly what the offeror proposed is called the *mirror image rule.* The acceptance must mirror the offer exactly. If the offeree says, "Okay, $1,000 for your car and an extra set of tires," he is making a *counteroffer* because it changes the terms. Many offerees do not accept the initial terms offered, and counteroffers are common. Technically speaking, when the offeree makes a counteroffer, the original offer is rejected and the counteroffer becomes a new offer, so the offeree becomes the offeror of a new offer.

The offeree can also reject the offer. This happens if the offeree is not interested in entering a binding contract. Rejections can be written, verbal, or implied (hanging up on a telemarketer). Sometimes an offeror may make an offer but then change his mind. An offeror may *revoke,* or withdraw, his offer at anytime until the offer is accepted. The effect of a rejection by the offeree or a revocation by the offeror is the same; the deal is dead.

Acceptances can be communicated to the offeror in any way the offeree wishes, but generally should be conveyed in the manner in which they were received or in a quicker manner. For example, I call the office supply store and offer to buy two reams of copy paper. The store clerk could accept my offer by saying, "Okay, we'll have it at the checkout with your name on it." Or he could call me back that morning after checking the supply and leave a message for me. Or he could fax me a confirmation later in the day. He probably would not want to send me an engraved acknowledgement in the mail, but he could. The law allows the acceptor to just indicate acceptance for it to be effective. This is called the *mailbox rule*. The law likes to interpret that an agreement between the parties has taken place as soon as possible, so once there is an offer and an acceptance, an agreement exists. So while the law requires the offeror to be specific and to ensure that the offer is actually received, the offeree may communicate acceptance in a much less secure way, like dropping a letter in the mailbox. The offeree has accepted the offer, but doesn't have to confirm whether it is received or not. This requirement makes business offerors pretty much expect that business offerees will accept the deal—and this approach keeps commerce moving.

Another way legal minds interpret "bargains to keep commerce moving" is by describing contracts as *unilateral* or *bilateral*. Those numerical terms refer to the promises that are made. If a contract is unilateral, there is one promise made. The deal is this: A promises to pay if B does some act (paints his house, sells him groceries, quits smoking, etc.). One person—the offeror—is making a promise and one person is performing an act, and only after the act is completed does the offeror have to "do his part" (pay the money). If you interpret "I will pay you $2,000 if you paint my house" as a unilateral contract, you have to paint my whole house before I owe you a penny, because I promised and you must act. I could walk out of my air-conditioned living room into the 110-degree heat you are working in and say, "I revoke my promise" while you are finishing the trim work on the last window, and legally, I would not owe you for your work. The bargain was for the whole house.

Unilateral contracts can be very unfair, so the preference is to interpret all contracts as bilateral contracts, or two-promise deals. If you interpret "I will pay you $2,000 if you paint my house" as a bilateral contract, I am promising to pay you if you promise to paint my house. Once the promises are exchanged, there is a deal (assuming all the other ingredients are present) and the action is complete. Therefore, I cannot renege on my half of the deal before the offeree is finished with the action. Bilateral contracts are considered fairer and more efficient in recognizing the bargain immediately upon the "meeting of the minds" to contract. Of course, there is still good use for unilateral contracts, and sometimes the offeror who is in control of the terms wants to specify that he requires completed action on the part of the offeree before he acts. For example, if I contracted for a custom-made gown to wear to my son's wedding, I would want to specify that I will not pay in full until I am satisfied with the workmanship and fit.

Consideration. The third ingredient in a binding contract is *consideration*. Consideration is not politeness, although polite business dealings are always encouraged. Consideration has a special meaning in the law and refers to the fact that the parties enter into a bargained-for exchange. This exchange of something of legal value distinguishes a binding contract from a gift. The something of legal value is often money, at least on one side of the deal, but money is not the only consideration given in contracts. The exchange could be an item for an item, or an item for some type of conduct. Consideration is doing something that you are not legally obligated to do. I am not obligated to go to work every day. I could sit home and eat bonbons, but I choose to exchange my daytime hours for payment from my boss. Consideration is also refraining from doing something you have every legal right to do. For example, my nephew is over 18 and has every right to smoke. I do not like smoking. I promise him $500 if he quits smoking for six months. He quits, and the only reason he does is because I made an agreement with him. He is giving up something he has every right to do specifically in exchange for my promise to pay him $500. If he quits for six months, I owe him $500. He has every legal right to collect that from me. I cannot say to him, "Ah, you should have quit anyway, and I did you a big favor." I have to pay.

Capacity. The next ingredient in a binding contract is *capacity*. The law restricts some individuals from making binding contracts. Minors cannot enter into binding contracts unless they are for necessities, like food and shelter. This law prevents disreputable individuals and businesses from taking advantage of minors who may not be mature enough to enter into contracts knowledgeably. In most states, minority terminates at 18 years of age. The law also protects those operating under a mental impairment from entering into binding contracts. Mental impairment does not relate to a certain IQ or age; it relates to whether an individual has an appreciation of the consequences of his actions. Often elderly or infirm individuals have questionable contract capacity, but so can healthy 30-year-olds after major surgery or during a significant illness.

Legality. The fifth ingredient in a binding contract is *legality*. The law will not enforce a contract for an illegal purpose. Therefore, contracts regarding prostitution, illegal gambling, and agreements to commit torts are not enforceable. Another type of contract that is lacking in legality is one that is contrary to public policy. These contracts would include agreements containing exculpatory clauses. An *exculpatory clause* is a provision that attempts to relieve one party from liability. A surgeon would be using an exculpatory clause if he asked his patients to sign an agreement promising never to sue him under any circumstances. This is different from signing an informed consent that a surgical procedure may be dangerous. An exculpatory clause would attempt to exculpate, or free, the surgeon from liability even if the surgeon was negligent in his care. Another example of a contract contrary to public policy is a contract that is so one-sided as to be unconscionable. An *unconscionable contract* is one that is outrageous or unscrupulous, usually because the parties have such unequal bargaining power that one party takes unfair advantage of the other. For example, a paycheck advance loan that charges 300 percent interest could be unconscionable, and thus, be challenged for legality.

Voluntariness. The final ingredient in a binding contract is voluntariness. *Voluntariness* refers to the conditions under which a contract is entered into. An elderly parent signing over the deed of his house to his son because of threats to "put the old man in a nursing home" if he doesn't, is not a voluntary agreement. Contracts that are entered into because of threats, force, or duress do not represent true agreement.

The law also will not enforce a mistaken, misrepresented, or fraudulent contract. A contract is mistaken if an important term in the contract is based on a mistake between the parties. This type of mistake does not mean that you changed your mind. This requirement will not relieve you from second thoughts about a purchase. This type of mistake refers to some fact that may affect the *agreement* part of the deal. For example, I have two cars, a 2004 Volvo and a 2004 Mazda Miata. I tell my coworker, "I am selling my car." He says, "How about $17,000 for your car?" I say, "Great. It's a deal." He thinks he bought the Volvo; I think I've gotten rid of the leaky convertible. There has been a mistake in our agreement that affects our voluntariness, or willingness to go ahead with the deal.

A contract is misrepresented if one party gives false information about a fact that may affect the agreement. For example, maybe my coworker and I were not thinking about different cars. We both intended our transaction to refer to the Miata, but before he offers me $17,000, he asks me if I have had any trouble with the convertible leaking. I say I have not, although that is the prime reason I am getting rid of it. This *misrepresentation* could affect the voluntariness of this bargain. My coworker would not have offered $17,000 for a leaky car, despite its sleek exterior. A contract is fraudulent if one party deliberately or intentionally misrepresents a fact about the subject of the agreement. When you make a fraudulent statement in a contract negotiation, you intend to deceive the other party. It could be fraud if I went on the say to my coworker, "The Miata has never leaked; you have nothing to worry about there." This clearly affects the voluntariness of the agreement, and if fraud is present, the contract can be voided or cancelled.

If all six elements of a contract are present and one party does not perform as promised, the injured party could sue in court for damages. *Contract damages* are calculated to give the injured party the benefits of the bargain and are discussed in detail in chapter 10. If you want very detailed deadlines in your agreement, put it in the agreement. If you want your contract to be interpreted as a unilateral contract, put it in your agreement. Contracts are between individuals in society, and freedom of contract is a basic, fundamental right reserved to the people by the Fifth and Fourteenth Amendments to the U.S. Constitution. Individuals and businesses are very free to enter into contracts about any legal subject. The law does not care if your contract is a good deal. The law will enforce a contract in which one party overpays for an item. The law does not care if your contract is silly. The law will enforce a contract to paint your kitchen with polka dots and pink flamingoes. So, the contracting parties set the terms that really control the deal.

Quasi Contract and Promissory Estoppel

Sometimes an ingredient is missing. You took some steps, did some work, paid some money, but technically you don't have a good contract. In this case, the law may give you some relief even though you goofed up. One thing the court may do is listen to an argument in *quasi contract*, or "almost contract." In this case, you throw yourself on the mercy of the court, admit that you were a little lacking in the recipe, but ask for some relief to avoid a terrible injustice. Sometimes you really miss quite a few ingredients to a good contract. In that case you may argue *promissory estoppel*, begging the court to *estop*, or prevent, the other party from denying the deal because you, the injured party, have significantly relied on this faulty bargain, and allowing the other party to get out of the agreement would unjustly enrich him. Quasi contract and promissory estoppel arguments are equitable remedies (see chapter 2) and the court is allowed to act, not because it is interpreting a legally enforceable agreement, but because it is preventing an unfairness. The classic promissory estoppel example is the roofing company that comes to your house and begins to put on a new roof, which you go out and watch them install, even though you know they meant to do the neighbor's roof. Significant value was given to you in a new roof. You could have spoken up and prevented the situation that has unjustly enriched you. Technically, there is no contract between you and the roofing company, but it would be an injustice not to provide the company with some relief—that is, money for the job. These noncontract arguments are brought to court more often than you may think, mainly because a lot of people try to do their own contracts without legal advice, goof up in the particulars, and then need help enforcing their rights.

THE LAW IN ACTION

Do the Buyers and Sellers have a legally enforceable agreement? Let's check the ingredients:

1. The Buyers made a written offer to the Sellers. It was clear and definite—123 Cherry Lane for $91,000. It was communicated to the Sellers through the Realtor. This was a bilateral agreement, completed when the offer to purchase was signed. The Buyers promised to buy and the Sellers promised to sell. The deal would be completed within one month, at the actual closing of the sale, but the promises binding the parties to the contract were made when each party signed the offer to purchase.

2. The Sellers accepted the offer. They thought about it for a bit, but they signed it and dispatched their acceptance by returning the signed offer to purchase. They did not change the terms and counteroffer a price of $95,000, although that is what they hoped to get initially. They accepted the offer that was made to them with no changes.

3. There was consideration. Consideration is a bargained-for exchange. The Sellers are selling their house, which they are not legally obligated to do. The Buyers are giving $91,000 of their money to the Sellers, which they are not obligated to do. Both are getting something of value.

4. Both the Buyers and the Sellers have capacity to enter into binding contracts. They are of legal age and there are no disabilities operating in this case.

5. The contract meets the requirement of legality. Buying and selling real estate is legal everywhere in this country.

6. It appears that this contract was voluntarily entered into. No one forced the Sellers to take this offer or to move in the first place. The Buyers certainly took their time and looked at this house on three occasions before deciding to make an offer.

The parties' respective positions vary. As far as the Sellers are concerned, there is a binding contract that the law should enforce. The Buyers should be made, by a court, to complete the transaction no matter what *issues* they have with the living room floor. After all, they are getting a great house. They can put down a rug or even install hardwood floorboards if they wish. The Sellers believe a court should award them damages in the amount of $95,000 if the Buyers don't follow through on the deal.

As for the Buyers, they are in shock. How could this have happened? Didn't they ask specifically about the floors? Were there ulterior motives at play when the Sellers would never be available to let them measure for curtains? If the Sellers lied about the floor, what other hazards lurk? Sure, there was an offer, acceptance, consideration, capacity, and legality, but not so fast on the voluntariness. The Buyers bargained for a house with hardwood floors in the living room, not plywood. At a minimum there was a mistake. The dealings probably point more to a misrepresentation or even intentional fraud on the part of the Sellers. The Buyers believe a court should not enforce this contract due to the lack of voluntary agreement. However, the Buyers admit that hardwood floorboards could be installed in the living room for about $2,200, which is about 2 percent of the purchase price.

Have you decided whom you are rooting for? Keep reading to discover the conclusion to this case in chapter 8.

TEST YOURSELF

1. David Doright has just buttered the fresh popcorn and grabbed his can of soda. He positions himself in front of the large screen television in his living room and tunes in to his favorite show, *Antiques Roadshow*. Tonight's program is from St. Louis, his hometown. Although it is strictly a hobby for him, David fancies himself pretty savvy about antiques. Halfway through the show, a small chest of drawers is featured. The owner, a young man, tells that he bought it about six months ago at a garage sale to furnish his first apartment. The chest looks familiar to David. As he leans in to get a better view, David realizes that this is the old chest from his basement, which he sold at his last garage sale for $20. David then hears the expert describe the chest as a rare George III piece worth $20,000. David chokes on his popcorn. Can David cancel this contract and get his chest back?

2. Judy starts her day with a piping hot cup of coffee from the vending machine in the lunchroom. Today, she puts in her dollar and out comes the aromatic vanilla cappuccino—right onto the floor and her new suede shoes. The cup failed to fall into place. Is this a breach of contract or a tort?

3. Sally's son, Rex, is an active boy. He is also quite big for a seven-year-old. Last Saturday, Sally was picking up a wedding present in the china shop, and while checking out, she let go of Rex's hand for just a minute. Crash! A lovely Waterford vase was smashed to bits. The owner has a clear sign at the entrance, YOU BREAK IT, YOU BUY IT. What happens next?

Brain Teasers

4.   Arthur Roberts is a famous architect. He is in demand to design unique houses for the rich and famous. Mr. Roberts just finished an eight-month-long project—a Malibu estate for Mr. and Mrs. Rock Star. At the closing today, the Stars refused to pay the balance due to Roberts of $560,000 because they just learned that Mr. Roberts let his architect's license lapse by failing to send in his renewal fee of $25 on time. The Stars are claiming that this is an illegal contract since Mr. Roberts was not legally licensed throughout the contract. Is the contract illegal, and thus unenforceable?

5.   Dan contracted with Eric to do the snow removal on his property this last winter. They agreed that for all snow removal needed from November though March, Dan would pay $200. Dan paid Eric in full on November 8. Through March 31, it only snowed two times. Can Dan ask for a refund? What if it had snowed 30 times last winter? Could Eric ask for more compensation? Could promissory estoppel apply here?

Question Future Chapters Will Answer

6.   What will happen to the Buyers and Sellers of 123 Cherry Lane? If the Buyers breach a legal agreement, what will the consequences be? Are there any defenses the Buyers could raise so they don't have to go through with this deal? In tort situations, there are some defenses that can be raised such as contributory or comparative negligence. Would this approach help here?

Answers can be found on pages 215–218.

KEY POINTS TO REMEMBER

- Contract law is a category of civil law concerning private rights between parties who make an agreement.

- Contracts come in many forms: written and oral, implied and express, executed and executory, and unilateral and bilateral. These are all terms that describe an aspect of the agreement.

- A contract is an agreement the law will enforce.

- The recipe for a binding contract is offer, acceptance, consideration, capacity, legality, and voluntariness.

- If you don't have all the ingredients to form a binding contract, you may have a gift, ethical obligation, sales pitch, or motivational promise, but not a legally enforceable agreement.

- If you have all the ingredients to form a binding contract, the law will protect you so that you get what you bargained for.

- To be sure you have a winning recipe for your contract, be sure to ask for all the extra ingredients that are important to you.

- If your recipe almost works, but falls short of an ingredient, the law may enforce your promises using an equitable remedy called promissory estoppel.

Contracts: Do You Always Have to Do What You Promised?

I recently had to replace the printer I use at home. I shopped around, looked at all my friends' printers, and even asked my 23-year-old son for advice. After considerable deliberation, I bought a name-brand model with a wireless feature from a big box electronic store. That was an easy contract. By the time I had done all the research, I just went in, pointed to the one I wanted, and checked out. Contract completed.

Then the trouble began. The printer was very hard to hook up and didn't function wirelessly. I hired a computer wizard to help with the setup. When he could get the printer to work, it was very slow—much slower than advertised—and it made a loud grinding noise in the process of printing. After two attempts at wireless hookup, I attempted to use the printer with a cable, and that was no more reliable.

I thought I knew what I wanted and needed in a home printer, but this is not it. I am not happy with my contract. The big box store claims in advertisements that they want satisfied customers, so they should not be happy either. Can I get out of my bargain? Can I get reimbursed for the bills I paid to the computer wizard?

IN THE REAL WORLD

In chapter 7, we met the Sellers and the Buyers. They entered into a legally enforceable contract to exchange ownership of a house for $91,000. The promises were made; the deal was done. All that was left was the official closing.

The night before the scheduled closing, the Buyers learned that the house was not as they expected. The beautiful hardwood living room floor was mostly plywood that had been covered by a rug. The Buyers are now questioning every assurance the Sellers made about the home. They want to back out of the deal but don't exactly know what that means. Can they be forced to buy the house? Can some nominal sum, like forfeiting the $1,000 down payment, get them out of the deal? Isn't there some kind of law?

It is clear that the Realtors (the one for the Buyers and the one for the Sellers) knew nothing about the floor "problem." The Sellers had told their Realtor that the house had "some hardwood floors," which was true, as one bedroom was carpeted and the kitchen was tiled. No one had pulled back the rug in the living room to look underneath. The Sellers did not offer the plywood information at any time, although they admit they were asked some general questions about the floors before the offer was made.

The Sellers have moved out. They have taken significant and substantial steps in reliance on this deal. From their point of view, the floor "problem" is minor compared to the great piece of real estate the Buyers are getting. Even the Buyers admit that they wanted an older home and with it, they expected some surprises. Well, here is surprise number one: In the 1920s, some houses were built with hardwood floors only at the edges of the rooms. Area rugs and this building feature were commonly used to save costs. It would take about $2,200 to put hardwood flooring in the middle of the room if the Buyers so chose. The Sellers know for a fact that the Buyers were going to spend this much on new drapes for the living room. Can the Sellers force the Buyers to buy the house? Can the Sellers keep the house and also get damages from the Buyers for breach of contract? How much can they get? Whatever happened to *buyer beware*? Isn't there some kind of law?

KEY CONCEPTS

Chapter 7 outlined the ingredients necessary to make a legally enforceable contract. Unfortunately, parties to a contract will not always do what they promise. Ideally, the way to complete, or *discharge*, a contract is to perform. Most contracts are discharged through performance. I buy my groceries, I go to work, and I make my mortgage payment every month. However, some contracts are not discharged as agreed. Just like in cooking, having all the ingredients doesn't necessarily mean that the recipe will turn out the way we expect.

Contract Breach

When a party fails to perform what he promised, he breaches, or breaks, the contract. This failure has consequences not only for the party breaching the deal but also for the injured party. If my neighbor, Philip, breaks his agreement to drive me to work today, he is the one who failed to perform, but as a consequence, I have to pay $3 to take the bus to work. My agreement with Philip is that I pay him $2 per day, so his failure has cost me $1.

As a general rule, the person breaking the contract should compensate the injured party by giving him the benefit of the bargain. In that case, I should not have to pay Philip for the transportation that I did not receive and I should get $1 from him to cover the extra costs I paid to take the bus. But, I also arrived late at work and that was a problem. I often am slow getting started in the morning and am usually late getting back from lunch. Today, when I was running in, the boss informed me that I would be getting a negative review this month due to tardiness, so no bonus for me. Can I sue my neighbor for the lost bonus that his missed ride caused? No, I cannot. Contract damages are limited to compensating the injured party for the benefit of the bargain, not for items that are not foreseeable or reasonably related to the deal.

The law is very liberal in the rules that allow parties to enter into contracts, so, in cases of breach of contract, the law does not award punitive damages, as it does in some tort cases. Adults and businesses are free to enter into any bargains they desire that are legal. If you make a bad contract, the law is not going to punish the other side with excessive damages. In my case, I should have a reasonable backup plan, which I do, with my $3 bus ride. If Philip proves himself unreliable repeatedly, I am free to contract elsewhere.

Discharge by Impossibility. Sometimes things happen that make a contract impossible to perform. Examples of impossibilities include the death of a party to a contract, the destruction of an item that is the subject of the contract, or an act of God. When a contract is legally impossible to perform, the contract is voided and therefore it is over.

If Kitty Carlisle had agreed to sing at my anniversary party for $5,000 but she died before the event, the contract is impossible to perform. This is a unique personal service. Even if Tony Bennett were willing to step in for Kitty, it wouldn't be the same. If I had paid, I would be entitled to my $5,000 back. If a party to a contract dies before it is fully performed and the contract does not involve a personal service, perhaps the contract can go ahead. For example, if I were buying a house from an elderly gentleman who died before the closing, the man's heirs could still sell me the house, if they wished, but the agreement between me and the deceased could be voided if the heirs wished to void it. If the man's house burned down before the closing, I could void the contract due to destruction of the subject matter of the deal. I need a house to live in, not a very empty lot even if it is offered with a large check from the insurance company for the home's value. Similarly, a contract can be voided by an *act of God*, which refers to a natural occurrence, such as a flood or tornado, that could not have been prevented or foreseen. When an act of God strikes, the subject matter of the contract is usually destroyed.

Discharge by Operation of Law. There are also a few specific laws that forgive performance of a contract. The first one is the statute of limitations. The *statute of limitations* is a procedural law that says a legal claim must be brought within a certain period of time. Most contract claims have a statute of limitations of 10 years. You must sue to enforce a contract within 10 years of the breach, or the cause of action is too stale. This law protects against ancient claims being brought to court where evidence is old and memories are poor. The other law that may forgive performance is the bankruptcy act. Certain debtors are discharged from performing their contract obligations if they are declared legally bankrupt.

Discharge by Rescission. Occasionally, both parties to a contract may change their minds. This is called a *contract rescission*. In effect, a rescission voids the deal. Rescission must be a mutual decision by the parties, not a one-sided backing out of the deal. Technically, when parties agree to *rescind* a contract, they enter into a new offer and acceptance, agreeing not to perform on their previous promises. The consideration for the rescission is their mutual nonenforcement of the original terms. In the case of a rescission, each party should be put back in the place they were before the contact was entered into, as if the deal had never happened. An example of a contract rescission could involve your choice of graduate school. If you were accepted at a school you liked and indicated you would attend, but then your number one choice accepted you, you and the first school may mutually agree that you will accept the new offer. The first school does not really mind since it has a waiting list of other candidates anxious to get in.

So, to recap, once you enter into a contract, you could perform it to its completion. That is a discharge by performance. You could be excused from performance because of a death, destruction, or act of God. This is a discharge by impossibility. You could be excused from performance because of the statute of limitations or due to a bankruptcy. This is a discharge by operation of law. Or you could mutually decide to cancel the deal. This is a discharge by rescission.

Specific Performance. In the rare instance where compensation for the benefit of the bargain is not satisfactory, the law will consider ordering the breaching party to specifically perform the contract. *Specific* *performance* is unusual because it is rare that monetary damages cannot take care of the breach. For the court to award specific performance, the case has to involve unique or rare items. If I had a contract to buy a Kurt Vonnegut drawing (yes, he was an artist as well as an author) for $2,500 and the dealer selling it changed his mind, I would not want to accept my $2,500 back. I want that particular drawing. There is not another one like it and I made a deal. The fact that the dealer got sentimental is too bad. The fact that Kurt Vonnegut died before the drawing was delivered to me, so that now its value is much higher, is also too bad for the dealer. Money cannot give me the benefit of the bargain. Only the item itself will do, and in rare, unique cases like this, the court may order the parties to complete the contract as made.

Substantial Performance. As discussed in chapter 1, the law does not require a person or business to be perfect. Sometimes things do not go as planned. There are contract rules that cover less than perfect performance. If you do all of what you promised, you get the benefit of your bargain. If you do most of what you promised, shouldn't you get most of what you bargained for? The law thinks that you should and exhibits this belief in the doctrine of *substantial performance*. If a person substantially performs on a contract, he does not do a perfect job, but he makes an honest and earnest attempt to perform completely. For example, my brother-in-law builds houses. He is a great builder and rarely has a complaint from clients. He has a solid reputation in the community for offering a fine product and excellent workmanship. If on the closing date for a house he has built, one thing remains incomplete—the kitchen door handles (18 of them) are not in due to a back order—has he substantially completed the house? Of course he has. The contract should be completed, he should be paid in full, and the contract should be discharged. He is going to provide the door handles when they arrive and install them in a workmanlike manner. No one should want to hold up a moving van, a loan commitment for the buyers, a construction loan to pay off for the builder, and the kids getting enrolled in their new school for 18 door handles. On occasion, a whole order does not come in as planned, but 80 percent of it can be delivered to the customer today and the rest in two days.

Contracting parties who have relied on the agreement since the time the promises where exchanged do not want to start over now. They want to make do, as well as they can, and get complete performance as soon as possible. Even if complete performance is not possible, in many contracting situations 80 percent performance is preferable to zero percent performance. In cases where perfect performance can never be achieved, the parties might agree to amend their contract to cover what can be supplied. For example, the seller would provide 80 percent of the order and the buyer would pay 80 percent of the purchase price. This is called an *accord and satisfaction*. The parties come to an accord, or agreement, and consider the contract satisfied.

Material Breach. On occasion, there is less than substantial performance. This is called a *material breach*, meaning significant breach of contract. Under these circumstances, one party gets significantly less than he expected in performance from the other party, such that, for all intents and purposes, the contract is breached and some damages are owed.

For example, I am moving my law office from one location to another and need some build-out services in my new location. I hire A & S, an improvement company, to wall off a large area into two offices, hang new doors throughout the space, install a check-in window in the reception area, and apply a fresh coat of paint to the space. All the work needs to be done in 60 days. We agree on a contract price of $3,800 and I pay an $800 deposit toward the cost of supplies. After 60 days, I have terminated my rental agreement at my former location, packed up all my office equipment and supplies, rented a moving van, and arranged for a hookup of all new utilities in the new location. A & S has removed all the old doors, put in a crooked window in the reception area that looks like it is from Ma and Pa Kettle's house, and put up half the drywall. It is moving day and the space looks worse than it ever has. A & S has not done a complete job, or even a substantial performance of the contract. Its actions constitute a material breach of contract. Because of the deficiencies, I do not have to pay the remaining $3,000 contract price since I have not received the work this represents, and I may have additional tort damages to claim against A & S because of the harm they caused to my business by breaching our agreement. A & S could argue that they are entitled to some consideration, meaning money, for the work that they did do; however, the work done falls so far short of the work promised that a court would probably not give them much more money for their efforts.

Defenses to Contract Performance

In considering defenses to contract performance, it is important to revisit the discussion of mistake, misrepresentation, and fraud, begun in chapter 7. When any of these events occur, the voluntariness of a contract can be questioned, but, on occasion, these events are also used to defend against the enforcement of a contract. It is not always easy to figure out if a mistake should negate the element of voluntariness or not. Since contract law does not protect against bad bargains, the parties to a deal have the obligation to be precise and clear about the terms they desire. A claim that "I didn't know that old book was a valuable first edition" will not defeat a valid contract. However, if the mistake is made because of a party's careless or intentional failure to disclose an important term, that may be used to defend against performing a binding agreement.

In contract law, the term *mistake* refers to a minor failure to disclose. The mistake can be unilateral or bilateral. In a unilateral mistake, one side to the agreement is wrong about a fact relevant to the contract. For example, I order a pair of shoes online, thinking they are leather. The advertisement appears to picture leather shoes, but there is no description of the materials. The shoes are actually polyurethane and very stiff. I made a mistake. In such a case I either make do—which means I keep the shoes and try to break them in—or I return them and the deal is rescinded. With a bilateral mistake, both sides are mistaken about some element of the bargain. My secretary orders legal-size plain envelopes. The supply store delivers legal-size window envelopes, which she accepts and pays for without examining. Both parties are wrong in their interpretation of the deal, and the contract is likely rescinded, with a return of product on one side and a return of payment on the other.

Misrepresentation can be innocent or a little more sinister. If you are selling your grandmother's old Buick, you probably believe you are accurate in stating, "She only took it out on Sundays to church." But grandma might have been a wild bridge addict, out every night of the week, popping wheelies and screeching tires to get to games on time. Your representation might not be accurate, but you believe that it is. This is an innocent misrepresentation. However, in the law, the word *misrepresentation* usually notes a false or misleading statement made with the intent to deceive. Usually the party making the statement knows that it does not square with the facts. Misrepresentations can be overly zealous guarantees like "This product will strip off seven layers of paint in five minutes." They can be careless statements like labeling a product "low fat" when it does not meet the Food and Drug Administration standards for a low-fat food. Misrepresentations can also be reckless or negligent statements like "Safe for children under 3" on a product with many small parts that children may choke on. So, sales pitches, or precontracting persuasion, are not part of the contract, but false, misleading, or reckless sales pitches could be so influential to the bargaining as to be considered a misrepresentation, which in turn, could negate a contract.

The key to considering whether a misrepresentation can be used to negate a contract is whether a party relied on it in making the deal. If a statement is material—that is, an important part of the deal—and it turns out to be false, perhaps the agreement should not be upheld. An example of a material misrepresentation is an employer telling an interviewee that the business will always have a strong presence in the local community even though he knows the business is set to move to Mexico in three months.

Fraud is a deliberate disregard of the truth. A person making a fraudulent statement in a contract negotiation is telling a lie for the purpose of inducing the other party to enter into the bargain. This lie could be the telling of an untruth, which is fraud by commission, or the concealing of a fact that should be disclosed, which is fraud by omission. Such intentional misinformation does cast doubt on the voluntariness of the agreement, and thus, whether there was a legally enforceable agreement in the first place. However, in the instance of concealing a fact that should be revealed, the fraudulent party could argue that everything that was disclosed was true and that it was up to the other party to the negotiation to ask all the important questions, so a failure to ask should not invalidate the deal. In this case, fraud can be used as a defense to a contract that was negotiated with false information or omitted information.

Fraud by commission occurred before Super Bowl XLI in January 2007, when more than 70 football fans bought tickets online. Unfortunately, these tickets were counterfeit and the fans were turned away at the gate. Fraud by omission occurred when a stockbroker intentionally misled an investor to invest in a stock that immediately lost significant value. The investor would not have bought the stock if the stockbroker had disclosed the risk factors present that he knew but withheld from his customer.

THE LAW IN ACTION

In the matter of the Buyers and the Sellers of 123 Cherry Lane, there is a contract that has not yet been fully performed because the closing has not taken place. With the discovery of the plywood living room floor, the Buyers don't want the closing to take place as planned. The house is still intact, so it is not impossible to perform this contract. No one has died and there has been no act of God; however, the Buyers would like to change their minds. They don't want the house as it is. Perhaps if the Sellers would reduce the price by an amount equal to the cost of installing hardwood flooring, then they could come to an accord and satisfaction.

But, the Sellers are not willing to do this. The Sellers feel that a deal is a deal and that this is a unique house. They are not willing to rescind the contract. In fact, they feel so strongly about the deal that they are threatening to sue the Buyers for specific performance of the contract. In other words, they want the court to force the Buyers to close on the house. The Sellers' fallback position is to ask for damages. Damages should give them the benefit of the bargain, which is, according to their figures, a $20,000 net profit from the sale of the house. If the house has to be put back on the market and resold, it may sell for less than the $91,000 the Buyers were willing to pay. In fact, it probably will sell for less now that it is sitting empty with all its flaws exposed. The Sellers will also incur the expense of keeping the house until it resells. These expenses include the mortgage payments, taxes, utilities, insurance, and yard maintenance. In other words, the Sellers could suffer thousands of dollars in damages if the Buyers are allowed to void this contract.

The Buyers could argue that they should not be forced to perform on the contract due to a material breach. To win on this argument they would have to convince the court that a hardwood living room floor was a very important term for them. This was an item on their "must have" list, but so was a yard for the kids and an older home. Everyone admits that the floor can be made to fit the Buyers' expectations with a $2,200 expenditure. Obviously, the Sellers will argue that this is a small item that is not material to the deal and a very minute portion of the purchase price. The Sellers would urge the court to rule that they had substantially performed on the contract, even if their performance was not perfect.

The Buyers can also argue a defense of mistake, misrepresentation, or fraud. As discussed in chapter 7, these points raise questions about the voluntariness of the contract, but it is possible for the Buyers to admit that there is a legally enforceable agreement here and that their consent to the deal was voluntary, but still raise these points as a defense to performance. To win this argument, the Buyers need to concentrate on the facts and circumstances that show intentional misrepresentation or even active concealment by the Sellers. Key points to their argument are the specific questions they asked the Sellers when viewing the home and the inability to view the home after making the offer to purchase.

Let's say that the Buyers refuse to close on the house. The Sellers could sue the Buyers for specific performance, asking the court to order them to buy the house. This is a unique and extraordinary remedy that the court may be unwilling to enforce against the Buyers. In the alternative, the Sellers could also ask the court to award them damages for the Buyers' failure to close on the deal. If the house is resold for $79,000 before the case gets to trial, the claim for specific performance would have to be dismissed because the house is no longer available for the Buyers to purchase, but the damages claim would still be before the court. With these facts, if the Buyers lose, they face damages in excess of $12,000 due to the difference between the purchase prices. If the Buyers win and prove misrepresentation or fraud that rescinds the contract, they would get back the $1,000 earnest money that they had paid the Sellers. The stakes are high for each side.

After a two-day trial, the judge rules in favor of the Buyers. The judge didn't go so far as to find fraud on the part of the Sellers, but she did find misrepresentation that was deliberate on the part of the Sellers and material to the Buyers. As is usual in contract cases, each side has to pay their own attorney fees, which amounted to about $3,500 each. Contracting is not for the faint of heart. Carelessness in business agreements can cost dearly, even if you win your case.

TEST YOURSELF

1. Calvin scraped the left rear panel of his car backing out of the garage. This made him mad, not because he hadn't done it before, but because he was hoping to keep this new Toyota in scrape-free condition. The next day, he got a repair estimate from Lang Auto Body Shops for $550. Calvin agreed to the estimate and scheduled the repair for the following week. In the meantime, Calvin's mother fell and broke her hip. He did not get the car in the following week, and he has been so busy with family obligations that six months have gone by. What can Lang do about the contract breach? How can the parties discharge this contract?

2. Lou and Linda were scheduled to be married on May 20 in Longview Park. When arranging the details with city hall, they discovered that Judge Judy was to perform the services on that day. Judge Judy fell ill on May 18 and arranged for Judge Joe Brown to substitute. He did, but then the newlyweds sued Judge Judy for specific performance. Will they win?

3. The Browns always have a golden retriever. Their first dog, Maggie, was a real sweetheart. She was in the family before the first child, Matt, came along. After Maggie passed on, Sadie was there to welcome Matt's brother, Mike, and sister, Alyssa. Sadie passed on last October and the family got Mocha. All the dogs came from the same breeder, who guaranteed satisfaction to the customer. Mocha was different. She was a real type A dog. She could not be trusted alone in the house uncaged. She constantly chewed on furniture and bedding. She growled and nipped at the kids. After six months and lots of effort, it was clear Mocha would not fit in. Can the Browns take Mocha back to the breeder and get their money back? What type of contract discharge would this be?

Brain Teaser

4. Roz has a contract to submit 10 cartoons a month to *The New Yorker* magazine. In return, she receives $2,500. There is no guarantee that any cartoon will be used in the magazine, but for each cartoon published, she receives an additional $2,500. Her contract states that the 10 cartoons are due by the 15th of the month and that failure to deliver all the cartoons for the month by that date is a material breach of the contract for which Roz will pay *The New Yorker* $3,000. April has been a very unfunny month, and by the 15th Roz only has nine cartoons to deliver. On April 17 she delivers the 10th. Has Roz substantially performed? Has she committed a material breach of her contract? What damages does she owe *The New Yorker*, if any? What if none of the cartoons from the April submissions were printed? What if the one submitted April 17 were printed?

Answers can be found on pages 218–220.

KEY POINTS TO REMEMBER

- Most contracts are discharged by being performed according to their terms. If a party substantially performs his promises, he has met his contract obligations.
- Sometimes the parties to a contract mutually decide to change a term and agree on another term. This is called an accord and satisfaction, which voids the original agreement and replaces it with another bargain.
- If a party to a contract fails to perform, she has breached the contract and could be liable to the other party for damages.
- Contract damages are calculated to give the parties the benefit of the bargain.
- Contract damages do not include punitive damage awards.

- A contract can be voided due to destruction of the subject matter of the contract, death, or an act of God. This is called discharge by impossibility.

- A contract can be legally unenforceable because of a statute of limitations or the bankruptcy of a party. This is called discharge by operation of law.

- If the parties to a contract mutually decide to call off the deal, the contract is rescinded. This is called discharge by rescission.

- If a party contracts for rare or unique items, the court may award him the item itself rather than damages for breach of the deal. This is a rare remedy called specific performance.

- If a party does not substantially perform, this is called a material breach, and the party breaching the contract may be liable for damages.

- Sometimes mistake, misrepresentation, and fraud can be used as defenses to performing a contract.

What Contracts Must Be in Writing?

We learned in chapter 7 that contracts can be oral or written. We also learned that there is no secret handshake that must be made to seal a deal, that there are no magic words that make a contract valid, and no dollar bills that have to be exchanged to make it stick. We reviewed examples of extremely informal agreements that make up contracts in our everyday lives, such as making a purchase from a vending machine or using an ATM. However, some bargains that you make are too important to handle informally. They involve great reliance or great expense. There are some categories of contracts that the law requires be put in writing for the parties' safety and for ease of resolving disputes, should they arise. There aren't many, but they are important to know.

WHAT'S AHEAD

- The Statute of Frauds: MY LEGS
- The Elements of a Written Contract
- The Parol Evidence Rule

IN THE REAL WORLD

Joel is so mad. He just completed his second year of law school and was looking forward to his summer clerking job in a law firm in his hometown. He worked at Stevens and Sissel last summer. When he was hired last May 10, old Mr. Stevens said he could work with the firm every summer until he was out of law school. Joel counted on this job to gain experience in research and some decent pocket money. However, old Mr. Stevens died last Christmas and the new managing partner, Mr. Sissel, just told Joel that he does not have a job there this summer. Can Joel enforce this oral contract that was supposed to last three summers? Joel now wishes he was a better student last year in Mr. Berman's contract class.

KEY CONCEPTS

The idea of requiring writing for some contracts is very old and dates back to a 1677 English law. The United States adopted this rule and requires contracts that have to do with MY LEGS to be in writing. Of course, MY LEGS is an acronym, one that I learned almost 30 years ago from my contracts professor in law school.

The Statute of Frauds

The statute of frauds sounds like it should be about fraud. It is, in a way, but the *statute of frauds* refers to laws about which types of contracts must be in writing to avoid fraud. First, it is important to understand how an oral contract can be subject to fraud.

If Lord Neuman and I, serf Ellen, had an oral agreement about splitting the revenue from the crops I grow every year, it could work out just fine if we were getting along and both had great memories. However, year to year, our recollection of the exact terms could fade. I could get greedy. Lord Neuman could want to get me out of his fields and get serf William in because he is stronger and younger and willing to take a smaller percentage. Lord Neuman could die and leave me to deal with his evil son, Edgar. If we have a dispute over terms, and the agreement is merely oral, the only way we can prove our case in a court of law is by our own testimony. That is no problem for Lord Neuman. He is very well spoken. I, on the other hand, am a serf, and going to court is a bit daunting for me. I could be perfectly exact in my memory of details but less than convincing in my oral testimony. Lord Neuman could have a personal relationship with the judge. It just could be unfair. A written document would be better evidence of our terms and it could be interpreted on its face—that is, by reading its contents, rather than by listening to our spin on the deal. Such situations developed as commerce grew in England in the late 1600s, and the formalizing of contracts with the potential for fraud became important.

Today, the statute of frauds requires six kinds of contracts to be in writing to be enforceable. If these contracts are not in writing, they still can be agreed to and enforced by the parties to the contract as long as things go well; but in the event of dispute, unless your contract is in writing, the court will not enforce your deal based on oral testimony. You will be limited to your writing, and if you have none, the court will not help you enforce your rights.

The *M* in MY LEGS stands for *marriage*. Contracts made in consideration of marriage must be in writing. In bygone times, this referred to contracts to exchange money—given by the wife's family—to the husband-to-be for his taking the daughter in marriage. Today, the same rules apply to *prenuptial* or *antenuptial agreements*. These contracts, which seek to limit the rights of the prospective husband or wife if the marriage fails, must be in writing to be enforceable.

The *Y* stands for *year*. Contracts that cannot, by their own terms, be performed within one year from the day after the contract is formed must be in writing to be enforceable. The reason these agreements should be in writing is that memories fade and parties change. (See chapter 10 about contract assignments.) I don't remember all the terms of my adjustable rate mortgage, which will last for the next 30 years. I know my bank and banker will change in 30 years. It is only prudent to have something as important as a long-term agreement in writing.

The *L* stands for *land*. Contracts that involve an interest in land must be in writing to be enforced. This makes sense too because an agreement involving land is usually the single most expensive contract that an individual enters into. Even if it is a contract to rent or lease land to live on, it is an important agreement and one that should be as complete and detailed as possible. If you are renting an apartment month-to-month, you may stay for longer than one year, but all you can expect is to stay through the next month. If you lease an apartment for two years, you can count on staying there as long as you meet your terms of the bargain, which usually involves paying rent and not having wild parties.

The *E* stands for *executors or administrators*. Contracts that involve executors or administrators must be in writing. An *executor* is the person who settles the estate of a deceased party. Technically, an executor is named in a will. If a person dies without a will, he will have an *administrator*. The executor's job is to collect all the money the deceased had coming to him, pay all his bills, and distribute the balance to whomever the deceased named in his will. The administrator does the same thing.

An example clearly indicates the reason for requiring executor's agreements to be in writing. Let's say Joe Farmer dies leaving 1,000 acres of farmland in Missouri to his son, Joe Jr. The deceased named his attorney, Peter Kroeger, to be his executor. Peter collects all the money that Joe has coming to him, including a wrongful death claim, because Joe was killed in an automobile accident. He pays all of Joe's bills and then distributes the balance of the estate, which amounts to $150,000, to Joe Jr. Needless to say, Joe Jr. is a little surprised. He was expecting much more, but Peter explains that there were a lot of fees to pay to the attorney who handled the lawsuit—who happened to be Peter's partner—and Joe Sr. had some bills that needed to be paid that amounted to a lot of money. In addition, the land, although great farmland, only sold for $100 an acre. Joe Jr. wants to see the documents. Peter tells him it is all oral. This will never do. An executor stands in a position of trust working for third parties. Everything that he does should be documented and aboveboard to avoid fraud. Therefore, the actions of executors' and administrators' dealings on estate matters must be documented in writing.

The *G* stands for *goods*. Contracts for the sale of goods valued at more than $500 must be in writing to be enforceable. This contract qualifies for special treatment because it involves a significant amount of money and unclear terms could lead to serious consequences for the parties.

The *S* stands for *sureties*. Contracts involving sureties must be in writing to be enforceable. *Sureties* are individuals who guarantee or promise to pay the debts of another. Let's say I am starting a business, and I need to go to the bank and get a loan for some start-up capital. I don't have a lot of *collateral,* or assets to pledge to pay back the loan, but I have one powerful "friend." I met Donald Trump once in an airport. He shook my hand and said he was sure I would make it in business. I think this should impress my banker, so I tell her that Donald Trump is sure I will be a success and—here I am stretching a bit—I am sure he would back me for what I need. Should my banker believe this? Probably not, because what was Donald Trump doing in a regular airport anyway? Doesn't he have his own jet, if not his own airport? No, my banker wants it in writing—not my writing, but the writing of the person who is willing to serve as the surety for me.

This is only fair. You ought to know if you are on the hook for anyone else, and it should be memorialized in more than just an airport conversation.

All the MY LEGS contracts need to be in writing to be enforceable in court under the statute of frauds. Remember, parties may enter into oral agreements about these kinds of contracts, and if all goes well during the contract, the agreements could be fully performed and discharged with no problem. A party gets in trouble however, when he wishes to enforce one of these kinds of contracts in court and has no documentation.

In that case, the contracts will be deemed unenforceable because they do not comply with the statute of frauds. A party to an unenforceable agreement who has given value to or relied on the contract may present an argument to court using the equitable remedy of quasi contract or promissory estoppel. For example, my neighbor agrees orally to sell me a strip of land between our houses for $2,000. He gives me the deed and I record it so that in the eyes of the law, I own the property, but I haven't paid him yet. If he sues me for $2,000, I could argue that a contract for land must be in writing. There is no writing here, so the statute of frauds prohibits oral testimony to prove the contract. My neighbor would technically be out of luck, and I would be using a rule meant to limit fraud to, in fact, commit fraud. The law would allow my neighbor to use the argument of quasi contract or promissory estoppel to recover his funds. He did something to his detriment, namely deeding me the property, in reliance on my promise to pay him $2,000, and it would be an injustice to allow me to become unjustly enriched in this fashion.

What Type of Writing Do You Need?

Once you have identified that the type of contract you are entering into needs to be in writing, the next question to raise is what type of writing does it have to be? There is no requirement that the writing be on high-quality legal-size paper. The writing can consist of forms, such as a *purchase order* and an *invoice*. It could be an estimate, a letter, a fax, or a receipt that shows the agreement between the parties and the terms.

On occasion, parties just use a short writing called a *memorandum of agreement*. One of the shortest written contracts in history was the agreement to build the *Queen Elizabeth* ocean liner. It consisted of a letter from the shipbuilder, John Brown & Co., Ltd., to Cunard Lines saying, in effect, we agree to build the *Queen Elizabeth* for five million pounds.

At a minimum, the writing should identify the parties to the agreement, the subject matter of the contract, and the consideration agreed to by the parties. Hopefully, the writing goes on to include every detail that is important to the parties in as clear language as possible. Since parties are relatively free to contract about any legal subject, it is better to put an item in than to leave it out, even if it seems obvious or picky. If time for performance is very important, put it in the contract. If the buyer of an item is not going to pay until he is satisfied with the product, put it in the contract. If assignability of the agreement is important, put it in the contract. Finally, the writing should be signed by the parties to show their agreement to this writing, as a contract evidenced by writing is only enforceable against the parties who sign it.

The parties should use as clear and unambiguous language as possible to facilitate understanding. Lawyers are getting away from the legalese that has dominated contracts, but there still are many *terms of art*, or phrases with special meaning in the law, that may confuse the parties. Don't sign an agreement until you fully understand what each part means. If an issue that has not been reduced to writing comes up at the last minute and it is important to you, take the time to write it down and put it in the agreement. Don't have side agreements or last-minute oral modifications. Once you write down your terms, the law assumes that you have written down all your terms. You cannot bring in oral evidence of the "one more thing" you agreed to at closing.

Courts will interpret the language of your contracts using the clear dictionary definition of the terms you use. If you mean something different or specialized, spell it out in the contract. Terms written into a contract control if there is a conflict with preprinted terms. Ambiguities are usually resolved against the party who drafted the agreement.

The Parol Evidence Rule

The *parol evidence rule* underlines the importance of writing down everything that is important in an agreement, because it prevents a party from introducing evidence of any oral agreements that change or vary the written terms. The court views the writing as the best evidence of the agreement and gives no credence to any changes, additions, or modifications that a party may say occurred. If those details were important to you, you should know enough to write them down. This rule is especially important for businesses to be aware of as they enter into contracts with suppliers or contractors. If quantity needs change, write them down. If job specifications change, write them down. If you are caught without the documentation, you will probably be barred in court from testifying to an oral agreement about the item. Failing to be diligent about this has cost many a business big money.

THE LAW IN ACTION

Joel thinks he has a contract for three summers' worth of law clerking, but all he has is an oral agreement from a party who is no longer available to confirm or deny any of it. Since Joel's agreement could not be fully performed within one year, this agreement should have been in writing to be enforceable. Joel can try to persuade Mr. Sissel that ethically he should hire him for the summer, or he could try to beg for a job, but he does not have a contract right to work for the firm this summer. If he had only listened better in contracts class, maybe he would have asked for a memorandum of agreement last year. Such a document could be interpreted according to its written terms whether Mr. Stevens is available to verify it or not.

TEST YOURSELF

1. Farmer Dan has always wanted to get his hands on Farmer Bob's
    40 acres that adjoin Dan's property. One Friday, at the town hall fish
    fry, Bob is going on and on about how he wants to sell out. Dan seizes
    the moment and offers Bob $60,000 cash for the acreage. Bob accepts
    and the parties write on a paper napkin the following: "Bob agrees
    to sell his 40 acres to Dan for $60,000 cash to be paid by Monday."
    They both sign their names to the back of the napkin. Is this a valid
    contract? Is it an adequate writing?

2. Mr. Doogan has decided to give up driving. His family has been
    encouraging him to do so for a year. He is reluctant, but he knows it
    is time. However, he feels good knowing that his teenage neighbor,
    Jeff, wants to buy his 1999 Buick. They make an oral agreement that
    Mr. Doogan will sell the car to Jeff's parents for $6,000. Jeff, after all,
    is a minor and cannot legally enter into a contract. (See chapter 7.)
    The exchange takes place. Mr. Doogan is happy enjoying his money
    in the bank, and Jeff is happy driving the Buick to high school. Is this
    contract legally enforceable? Does it matter?

3. Time has flown by and Jeff is now 21. He is ready to ditch the Buick
    and get a car befitting his cool image. He has found a great 2005
    Mustang to his liking at Lee Motors. He can trade in the Buick and put
    down some cash he has saved from his job, but he still needs a loan
    for $12,000 to cover the difference. Jeff does not have much of a credit
    history at 21, so the bank is asking him to have his parents guarantee
    the loan. Jeff's parents agree to guarantee the debt, but they are
    out of town for the week and Jeff is anxious, so he forges his parents'
    signatures on the loan documents and returns them to the bank. Are
    Jeff's parents liable as guarantors of this loan? Why or why not?

Question Future Chapters Will Answer

4. George works part time at a grocer in the produce department while
    attending college. In his business law class, George just learned that
    contracts for the sale of goods in excess of $500 value must be in

writing to be enforceable, and all the important terms should be in the writing with no last-minute oral changes or modifications. George knows for a fact that Food Fair is always changing orders with their produce suppliers. For example, last week the store ordered 10 crates of bananas and 10 crates of pineapples, but the supplier delivered 12 crates of bananas and 8 crates of pineapples. Sometimes the supplier substitutes a different fruit than what was ordered or sends something extra. Are these written purchase orders any good? Should George be accepting these shipments that are not what the contract outlines?

Answers can be found on pages 220–221.

KEY POINTS TO REMEMBER

- The statute of frauds requires certain types of contracts to be in writing to be enforceable.
- Contracts that must be in writing (MY LEGS) include the following:
  - Contracts in contemplation of *marriage*
  - Contracts that take more than one *year* to be completed
  - Contracts regarding *land*
  - Contracts involving *executors or administrators* of estates
  - Contracts for the sale of *goods* with a value in excess of $500
  - Contracts involving *sureties,* or guarantors
- If a contract is reduced to writing, all the important terms should be included in the writing.
- If a contract that should have been in writing is not in written form, the court will not enforce it because it violates the statute of frauds.
- Interpretation of written agreements will be based on the ordinary meaning and common usage of the words in question.
- If a contract is in writing, the court will not listen to oral testimony about changes or modifications of terms that don't appear in the writing.

What About Me? Third-Party Rights in Contracts

In today's fast-paced business environment, you can open a bank account one day and by the time you get your ATM card, you can be dealing with a completely different entity. Due to mergers and corporate takeovers, my bank has changed names four times in the last two years. My car loan is not held by the original lender and my mortgage payment goes to some post office box in South Dakota. I've never been to South Dakota. Do I have anything to say about this "sleight of hand" going on with my documents? Do the new parties I am dealing with really know the terms of the bargain I struck? Why is this so prevalent?

WHAT'S AHEAD

- Third-Party Beneficiary Contracts
  - Intended Beneficiaries
  - Incidental Beneficiaries
- Assignments

- Assumptions
  - With Release
  - Without Release
- Powers of Attorney and Proxies

IN THE REAL WORLD

Virginia's parents bought her a life insurance policy when she was three months old. They thought it was a financially responsible thing to do and it was quite inexpensive to insure Virginia's life for $10,000. They named themselves as beneficiaries of the policy and as the alternate, they named Virginia's legal heir. The policy was paid up and thrown into a drawer decades ago. Virginia died last month at the age of 85. Both her parents died years ago. Virginia is survived by her husband, Walter. She had no children. Who gets the life insurance money and how do they claim it?

KEY CONCEPTS

Contract law is about private parties making bargains. For the most part, the law won't impose itself into the deal but rather will leave the parties to set out the terms that are important to them. Contract law doesn't generally let third parties intrude into others' deals either. For example, if my sister gets an awful haircut from the salon, I can't go barging in and demand a refund. It's none of my business, even if it is painful for me to see her with that mullet.

Third-Party Beneficiary Contracts

There are some types of contracts that, by their nature, involve three parties, and the law will allow the benefited party to have some rights in the bargain.

The simplest type of contract that benefits a third person is an insurance agreement. The insurance company is the *promisor* that agrees, upon a death, to pay out money. The *promisee* is the owner of the policy or the one who purchases it and pays the premium. The third party who benefits from this contract is the *intended beneficiary* whom the promisee has named to obtain the *proceeds* from the promisor when he dies. This arrangement is basically a gift. The beneficiary who receives the insurance proceeds does not make the bargain or give any consideration for the benefits he receives, but he is intended to benefit from the deal. If the insurance company does not pay out on the policy, this intended beneficiary has rights to sue for enforcement of the contract. The intended beneficiary does not have rights to sue under this contract until his interest vests, or becomes due. So, if I decide to cancel a life insurance policy I have, the beneficiary that I have named cannot object and force me to keep it in place. I am still free to modify my own contracts without the consent of the beneficiary, but if I die with the insurance in place, my beneficiary can inject himself into this contract and sue for the proceeds.

On occasion, a person may have a high interest level in a contract that does not concern him. This is an *incidental beneficiary*. Mere incidental interest does not grant you rights to sue under an agreement to which you are not a party. For example, I live in Davenport, Iowa, on the east side right next to Bettendorf. The City Council of Bettendorf has proposed to build new tennis courts in Williams Park, which is about four blocks from my home. I would love to have new, lighted tennis courts so close. In fact, I am planning my summer activities now and those tennis courts play a big part in my plans. If in the coming weeks the City of Bettendorf scraps that plan, can I sue to force the city to meet my expectations? Unfortunately, I can't, even though I am really, really interested in this project. I am only an incidental beneficiary of this deal. I have not made a promise of my own or offered consideration such that I am bound to any part of the bargain. Incidental beneficiaries, even if they are quite interested, cannot sue to enforce bargains that only indirectly benefit them.

Assignments

On occasion, a third party may get involved in a contract because of an *assignment*. This occurs when either the original promisor or promisee of a contract wishes to be relieved of his obligation and substitute a new party in his place.

This also usually relates to contracts that are executory in nature, or performed over time. For example, Ron purchased his car two years ago from Big Toyota dealership. He could not pay for the car all at once, so he got a loan from First Bank. First Bank gave him 80 percent of the purchase price and he paid 20 percent of the purchase price from his savings. To drive the car off the lot, Ron paid Big Toyota the full purchase price for the car. His contract with the dealership is fully executed and discharged, but his agreement with First Bank to pay back $20,000 is ongoing and will be performed over the next 36 months. This is an executory contract and either the promisor or the promisee could be interested in assigning his rights to a third party. Whether assignment is permitted or not is up to the parties of the contract. Most written contracts specify whether interests in them may be assigned or not. When oral contracts are in question, state law and case precedents determine whether they can be assigned.

In the above example, Ron may want to assign his interest in this contract with the bank if he wishes to sell his car before the loan is fully paid. Of course, if Ron wishes to sell the car within three years, the simplest way to do so is to ask for enough money to pay the bank loan off and sell the car outright to a third party. However, sometimes the third party does not have all the cash to do this. If Ron needs to sell the car soon after the purchase and the buyer could pay 20 percent of the price in cash, an easy way to complete the deal would be to let the third party substitute for Ron with the bank. Ron could be out of this deal, nice and clean. But the bank would have something to say about that. The bank was one of the original promisors to the contract, and it promised to loan the money to Ron based on his credit, his income, and his financial abilities to pay the money back. The bank does not have to settle for doing business with anyone Ron may choose to substitute into the bargain, nor does it have to offer the same deal to the third party. For this reason, most written contracts prohibit assignment on the part of the promisee.

To determine whether oral contracts are assignable or not, statutes and case law generally focus on the nature of the contract. Personal service contracts are not assignable. It does make a difference whether Wolfgang Puck caters your wedding reception or if Joe's Tavern shows up with a keg. Bargains for services are specialized and often unique. However, contracts in which the parties did not rely on the personal services of the other party or the performance of a unique skill, could be assigned. This is different from the situation with Ron and First Bank where Ron's particular financial abilities were part of the bargain. An example of an acceptable assignment of an oral contract would be if Debbie ordered a dress online and the company which usually ships via Federal Express shipped her order Priority U.S. Mail because of a workers' strike.

Promisors usually stand in a freer position than promisees when it comes to assignment. Promisors generally reserve the right to assign their side of written agreements, and oral agreements are usually interpreted to allow promisors to assign their interests. This is because promisors usually collect payments. It does not matter to Ron if he makes his monthly payments to First Bank or State Bank or Citibank, as long as the loan is paid off in three years. So promisors often assign their interests in a contract to third parties that step into their shoes.

Third parties that are assigned the rights to a contract can only get what the *assignor* had. In other words, State Bank cannot call Ron's loan due in two years and Citibank cannot up the interest rate to 12 percent. An *assignee* only gets what the assignor had to give. The underlying agreement stays the same. This is true of the rights under the agreement, such as to receive the monthly payment, and it is also true of the obligations under the agreement, such as to send monthly notices to the customer and to send additional notices if payments are late.

Assignment of loan documents is so popular because it is a financial tool for businesses. Many banks and financial institutions have lending restrictions that require them to keep a certain percentage of liquid assets. If a bank is aggressively lending its assets, it could be "loaned up" and unable to meet demand. To rectify this problem, a strong secondary lending market has developed over the last 25 years. For example, a bank may package a group of 100 loans, representing $2,000,000 to be paid over the next three years at 6 percent interest and sell them today, at a discount, to a secondary lender for cash. This gives the bank more money to loan out now, and the sold loans provide a predictable return for the secondary lender. Banks and financial institutions package mortgage loans, consumer loans, auto loans, and business loans for sale on the secondary market. Some businesses bundle their accounts receivable and sell them to investors at a discount to raise cash. This practice, called *factoring*, is a common tool to increase liquidity. In both secondary market sales and factoring, there is an assignment of the rights and interests of the seller to the buyer. The seller can offer only the rights she has and the buyer can exercise only the interests the seller had in the original agreement; but the transaction results in a substitution of parties such that the contract no longer involves one of the original parties. When the original promisee pays off his obligation to the promisor, the release of the debt or "paid" loan document comes from the third party that now holds the rights to the contract.

Assumptions

Assumption is also a term used in the law, which implies that a third party has stepped into a contract. An assumption is the act of taking on the obligation of another.

Assumptions are not different from assignments; they are just the other side of the same coin. The original contract promisor assigns his rights in a contract to a third party and the third party assumes the obligation. It almost sounds like an offer and acceptance—the two steps in forming a contract in the first place—and it is a bit like that. Not only does the original promisor have to turn over, or assign, his rights to a third party, but the third party also has to acknowledge, or accept, being placed in the position of the promisor to the original promisee. Therefore, to accomplish an assignment, there must be two documents, and all three parties need to be involved. Sometimes the assignment and assumption is combined in one document signed by all three contracting parties. Assumptions, like assignments, can only apply to the rights that the original party had. Assumptions are not opportunities to change the terms of the original agreement.

It is most important for all parties involved in an assumption to be clear on whether the agreement is an assumption with a release or without a release. An *assumption with a release* means that the new party to the deal is now the promisor to the original promisee. In other words, the third party has replaced the promisor in the agreement and the original promissory is off the hook. If the contract is not performed properly in the future, the only recourse the promisee will have is with the third party.

An *assumption without a release* is an agreement by the original promisee to add a party to the agreement, and look to that third party first for performance, but it does not let the original promisor out of the deal. If the contract is not performed as it should be, the promisee may still sue the original promisor, or the new third party, or both, for damages.

Assumptions of mortgage loans were very popular in the 1980s when interest rates were very high. Most mortgage loans at that time allowed assumptions of the contract. Buyers were reluctant to go out and sign up for new mortgages with 12 percent or 13 percent interest for 30 years, so they were anxious to assume the mortgages that the sellers already had at fixed rates of interest that were much lower. Of course, the buyers of homes had to come up with the difference in price between the mortgage balance and the selling price of the home, but in high inflation times, it is a buyer's market and even sellers who had been in their homes for a few years had not paid down significantly on the mortgage principal. Often, sellers were so anxious to sell that they would offer to take a second mortgage on the real estate, in effect giving the buyers time to pay off their proceeds, too.

Mortgage companies had a strong interest in who was coming into the contract agreements. So even though the mortgage documents might have allowed an assumption, the lender had to be involved and evaluate the new party to the bargain for their creditworthiness. If the buyers had strong financial statements, banks would offer an assumption with a release of the original *borrower*. This was preferable, because often the original borrower was off to Alaska or some distant shore and would not be around to collect from anyway. One good customer was just as good as another. However, if the buyers did not have much credit history or would not qualify on their own merits, the bank could still offer an assumption, but one without a release. This kept the original borrower on the hook in case the new third party failed to perform, but it let the original borrower go off to Alaska without the primary obligation to keep paying this mortgage each month.

Most who entered into assumptions without a release never heard from the original lenders again. The buyers did what they promised. Of course, some who were not released had unpleasant surprises, maybe years later, but a promise is a promise.

Powers of Attorney and Proxies

Powers of attorney and proxies are also agreements that involve third parties, but they are not third-party beneficiary contracts. Powers of attorney and proxies are documents that allow a third party to stand in for one of the contracting parties and exercise his rights for him. Powers of attorney and proxies do not allow third parties to take the place of the promisor or promisee in the original contract.

A *power of attorney* is a document that grants a party the power to stand in for another. The term *power of attorney* also refers to the person granted this authority. Powers of attorney are used when people are unavailable or unable to act for themselves. If Rick Steves is leaving for Europe tomorrow but his new house is scheduled to close the day after, he may need someone to represent him at the closing.

He could sign a power of attorney document and name someone to be his agent at the closing to sign papers, accept keys, and do anything else Rick would need to do if he were there. If a relative is aged or infirm, she may give you a power of attorney—that is, sign a form allowing you to be her representative at the bank—so you can deposit and withdraw funds for her and pay her bills. Giving a power of attorney to someone is not a sign that you cannot handle your own affairs. It is an agency relationship and every so often anyone can need an agent.

Since the power of attorney document must be in writing (see chapter 9), it not only names the individual or individuals to act for you, it also outlines just what you want and need the person to do. *Plenary* powers of attorney give the agent authority to do any and all things that the individual could do herself. Do not give someone a plenary power of attorney lightly. He could clean you out. Limited powers of attorney may define a certain time frame or a certain issue for which the agent can perform for the principal.

For example, I could give a limited power of attorney to my brother to supervise my yard landscaping while I am on vacation. He could stand in my shoes and tell the landscapers what I want and answer questions for me if they arise. My brother is not assuming financial responsibility for the project. He is not a substitute in the deal for me. He is just my agent for two weeks. Neither should my brother direct the workers to put in a fishpond and a waterslide. A power of attorney must act on the principal's instructions, not exercise his own wishes or judgment on the issue at hand.

Powers of attorney have become very popular for heath care purposes. In fact, if you go to the hospital to have a splinter removed, they will probably ask you if you have a power of attorney. If you give someone your power of attorney for heath care decisions, it should be someone who knows what your wishes are. In acting for another as his power of attorney, your charge is to do what he would wish, not what you would prefer.

A *proxy* is a document that is similar to a power of attorney. A proxy names a person to act for the party signing it. It generally grants power to do a specific act for the principal. The word *proxy* refers to the person appointed and the document itself. In World War II, many couples got married by proxy. If one party to the marriage was away in the service, he could choose someone to stand in for him at the wedding ceremony and sign the marriage license on his behalf. Sophia Loren and Carlo Ponti were married by proxy in Mexico. Neither party was present for the ceremony.

Proxies are also used in corporate settings, especially to cast votes at annual shareholders meetings. If a small shareholder does not plan on attending the meeting, she can designate a proxy to vote her shares at the meeting. Proxies may allow the principal to tell the proxy how to vote or they may generally grant the proxy power to cast the principal's votes using his own discretion. Proxies are also used in companies to allow a designated individual to speak for another at a meeting.

THE LAW IN ACTION

At the time the policy was purchased, Virginia's parents thought it would benefit them. Parents often buy insurance on children because it is cheap, and if the unthinkable happens, they will have funds for a proper burial. Virginia's parents have died, so when their rights under the policy vest, or become due, upon Virginia's death, they are not available to take the proceeds as the beneficiaries. As is common in insurance contracts, they named an alternate beneficiary to take the proceeds if the primary beneficiary is unavailable to do so. The alternate beneficiary is Virginia's heir. She has no children.

In most states, Walter, as her surviving spouse, is her heir and entitled to the insurance proceeds. Walter may never even have known about the contract, but he now has rights to enforce the bargain Virginia's parents made almost 85 years ago. He is the intended beneficiary of the money and can claim it by showing Virginia's death certificate, the death certificates of her parents (who are not available as beneficiaries), and proof that he is Virginia's heir.

Even if you are never a third-party beneficiary of another's contract, it is important to understand this legal point because in your business dealings you may need to work with third-party contracts, and you don't want to pay the wrong person.

TEST YOURSELF

1. Fritz hired P. J. to paint his house this summer. P. J. started the house, but two weeks later, she had to have an emergency appendectomy. She will be laid up for two months. She has a colleague, Bruce, who has some extra time and is willing to step in for P. J. and finish painting Fritz's house. Fritz and P. J. had an oral agreement and Fritz has already paid P. J. in full for the job. Is this contract assignable?

2. Fritz wanted his house painted because his only daughter, Julia, is getting married in a backyard ceremony in September. The reception is at the home, but Fritz has contracted with The Outing Club, the oldest, fanciest country club in town, for the food. On August 30, Joseph, the main chef at The Outing Club, resigns and accepts a job at The Golf Club. Can Joseph assign this contract to The Golf Club and have them cater the reception?

3. Mom needs a hip replacement. She signs a power of attorney document naming her son, Buster, as her power of attorney for health care decisions. She tells Buster the night before she goes in for the surgery that she wants everything done that can be done to make this surgery a success and keep her alive. About one hour into the surgery, the doctor comes to Buster in the waiting room and reports that all is going well, but Mom needs some donated blood to keep up her blood pressure. The doctor wants Buster's permission to do this. Buster does not believe in blood donations and transfusions. What should he do?

Brain Teaser

4. JoAnn Smith received a refund check from her eye doctor for $250. She had made a deposit on an eye exam that was covered by her insurance. This was a nice surprise as JoAnn just told her college-age son, James, that she would make a $250 deposit into his local checking account so he could buy books for this term at college. Can JoAnn assign her rights in this check to James? How? Does the bank have to accept it?

Answers can be found on pages 221–222.

KEY POINTS TO REMEMBER

- A principal can direct his proxy to perform in a specific way or the principal may leave the decision-making up to the proxy's discretion.
- Some contracts are intended to benefit third parties.
- Intended third-party beneficiaries of contracts have rights to sue, get information, and demand performance of contracts that benefit them.
- Incidental third-party beneficiaries of contracts do not have rights to demand the performance of a contract, even if the contract interests them or they feel the deal will impact them.
- It is possible to bring a third party into your contract to represent you, such as a proxy or power of attorney. This delegation of your authority, which must be in writing, really gives the third party no personal rights in the contract.
- It is possible to assign the benefits you may receive under a contract to a third party.
- You can assign only the rights that you have in a contract; you cannot change the deal.
- It is possible for someone to assume the rights you have in a contract.

- A person can assume only the rights that the original party has in the contract; he cannot change the deal.
- Assumptions of contracts can be with release or without release of the original party.
- The term power of attorney can refer to either a document or a person who stands in the position of another.
- The designated power of attorney should act as the principal would in the situation at hand and not exercise his own wishes.
- The term proxy can refer to either a document or a person who stands in for another in a corporate setting, either to speak for the principal or to vote for the principal in meetings.
- A principal can direct his proxy to perform in a specific way or the principal may leave the decision-making up to the proxy's discretion.

CONTRACTS IN BUSINESS

Using the contract knowledge from the previous section, we now are going to look at some specialized types of contracts. Part III will concentrate on contracts used in business every day. First, sales contracts will be reviewed and we will discuss why some contract rules need to be relaxed between merchants in the fast-paced commercial world.

Next, we will review contracts that offer warranties and review what rights consumers have against manufacturers, distributors, and sellers. Then, we will look at deals involving security, in which a promise to repay a business debt is not enough and the creditor needs something extra to protect his interests.

Sales Contracts and Remedies for Breach

If you have read straight through this book and have just finished the multiple chapters on contracts, you are probably wondering how you lived so long without major legal problems. If you really get into the subject, there are so many details and rules about contracts that it could drive a person crazy. How does anything ever get done? Luckily, most people enter into agreements with the intention of performing them as promised. But there still are an awful lot of specifics to follow. How can businesses do their brisk trade every day with requirements like the mirror image rule and the mailbox rule? The answer is they can't and they don't have to. Contract rules are eased a little between those "in the business," and in this chapter we will analyze how sales contracts keep commerce moving.

WHAT'S AHEAD

- The Uniform Commercial Code
- Article 2: Contracts for the Sale of Goods
- Review of Contract Damages
- Contract Damages in Sales Transactions

IN THE REAL WORLD

Rose just opened her flower shop. She is ordering cut flowers from a regional wholesaler, Bonnett. She just placed her first order for 12 dozen roses in assorted colors and 12 dozen green-and-white carnations for St. Patrick's Day. She faxed the order to the wholesaler's main office in another town on her letterhead. Bonnett just faxed back a shipping order. It does not include a price per dozen, but indicates they are at the "market" rate. Rose has taken business law and knows that offers must be accepted on their exact terms and that the subject matter must be detailed. Is a shipping order an acceptance? Is "market" rate an exact price? Has she placed this order or not? St. Patrick's Day is four days away, and Rose is getting nervous.

KEY CONCEPTS

Contract rules are important. They give everyone an even playing field. I know I am not going to be bound to sell my car if, in a fit of rage over the muffler falling off, I offer it to Shelia for $100. I know that if my son puts up a lemonade stand in the front yard, offering a cool drink for 50 cents, that the neighbor can't sue him if he runs out of juice. The sign was only an advertisement, not an offer. I know that if someone does not perform her promises as agreed, I could get damages to give me the benefit of the bargain. Many of these rules are common sense, and even though every citizen doesn't know them by memory, contracting works pretty well on a day-to-day basis in this country.

Businesses contract hourly. Every day is filled with needs to buy, sell, order, and ship. Often a business works with the same suppliers and distributors repeatedly. They develop a routine and a flow in their business. They use a shorthand that is necessary to keep commerce going. This streamlining is wanted and needed, but a few rules are still needed to give everyone an even playing field. Enter the Uniform Commercial Code.

The Uniform Commercial Code

Early in the history of this country, the states were quite independent. They could coin their own money and set their own tariffs. This wasn't workable for long so our founding fathers provided in the U.S. Constitution that the federal government would be responsible for coining the money and providing the rules for interstate commerce. This helped merchants in Boston know how to get their products to Baltimore. However, there were still issues of intrastate commerce that each state regulated within its borders. Also, contract laws differed from state to state, as did common law, or court opinions about interpreting contract terms.

For private citizens, this mishmash of state laws didn't make a big difference. In the 1940s you still went to the local hardware store for your furnace filters, the grocer for vegetables, and the butcher for meat. But for merchants, it was fast becoming an intimidating maze. So, in 1952, after more than 10 years of debate, the first *Uniform Commercial Code* was published as a joint project of the American Law Institute and the National Conference of Commissioners on Uniform State Laws. The Uniform Commercial Code, known as the UCC, is not law. It is a compilation of rules that legal scholars suggested be adopted by states to make commercial dealings uniform and predictable. The proposed rules, organized into articles, recognized the similarities in the states' laws about contracting, tried to incorporate the habits businesses had developed in their day-to-day dealings, and dealt realistically with common problems occurring in everyday commercial transactions. Over time, each state legislature has adopted the UCC, but not in identical versions. Each state is free to adopt only the items of the code that they wish.

Article 2: Contracts for Sale of Goods

Article 2 of the UCC concerns the sale of goods, such as a car, a coat, or a compact disc. It does not concern the sale of services, nor does it apply to real estate purchases or leases. To interpret service and real estate contracts, you still need to look to statutes and common law for guidance. All states and the District of Columbia have adopted Article 2 in almost identical versions.

Article 2 eases up on many of the statutory or common law rules to allow easier, faster, and more predictable business dealings. This is especially appreciated by merchants, or those in the business of dealing in a particular type of goods, because they probably have developed a shorthand they use with their regular suppliers and distributors anyway. In common law, the offer and the acceptance terms of a contract have to be identical. This is the *mirror image rule.* It is a good rule to keep people from being bound to terms that one party may "slip into" the negotiation. But how many businesses read every word of a purchase order faxed to them before they respond with their own preprinted invoice or shipping receipt? Such detailed review of forms is not practical. It is also not practical to create an individual acceptance to each kind of offer you get in business. Everyone has his own format for purchase orders, with items he needs on his forms for his own tracking, accounting, etc. The UCC provides that acceptance can be made in any reasonable manner to show assent, even if there are some additional terms included, such as your internal file numbers and tracking information.

In common law, a contract will fail to be formed if the parties are not detailed and specific about the subject of the contract. Under Article 2, contracts can have *open terms*, such as no specified price, and still be valid. This does not mean that a seller of No. 2 pencils can charge $20 a pencil. When a price term is left open, the code provides that the parties mean a reasonable price. Why would a company order products with an open price term? Because it needs the 500 component parts it puts in its product, and will pass on the cost in its own pricing later. The UCC also allows parties to enter into *requirements* (send me all that I require) contracts and *output* (send me all you can make) contracts that are less specific than necessary under common law.

Article 2 also changes the common law *mailbox rule*. Under that rule, acceptance of an offer was effective the minute it was dispatched, such as being deposited in a mailbox. The acceptance was effective against the offeror even if it was never received. This was a good rule because it anticipated that offers would be accepted, and made an offeror plan on proceeding with the bargain. In day-to-day business, we want even more of an assumption that deals are made to be performed. Per Article 2, an acceptance does not even need to be dispatched. A contract can be accepted by just promising to perform it or by just shipping the item. For example, if Walgreens faxed an order to Wrigley's for 500 boxes of chewing gum, Wrigley's could dispense with the faxed acknowledgement and acceptance and just go ahead and ship the order. They are not required to call back or fax a promise to ship. This procedure gets things moving as fast as possible and foregoes an official acceptance.

Article 2 even allows the acceptance of an offer to be for additional or different terms from those ordered. For example, Deere & Co. may put in a rush order for 5,000 Number 553 bolts to Bolts, Inc. Unfortunately, the company just shipped its last available Number 553 bolts to Mitsubishi, but it knows that Deere & Co. can use Number 552 bolts to complete its job with no problem. It fills the order with Number 552 bolts for a number of reasons: It wants the business, it knows these will work, Deere knows these will work, everyone stays happy. In business, this works.

Merchants can even modify the contract terms and maintain a valid agreement. For example, my fabric store orders 50 bolts of various Halloween fabrics on August 30 for delivery on September 5. My distributor only has 40 bolts on hand but will get more on September 10. Both of us want the deal to work. He wants the sale and I want the fabric. Even if I can only get 40 bolts by September 5, I'll take them and he knows that I will. So, the distributor ships 40 bolts now and 10 bolts on September 10. All the sewing mothers and future goblins are happy with their selection, and well before the holiday I will have what I need for the season.

The UCC does provide some safeguards against sellers just sending any old thing to fill an order. Buyers have rights to limit acceptance of additional or modified goods within time limits, which puts the onus on buyers to inspect their products in a timely fashion. In addition, the UCC does not change the extreme freedom of contract that the law allows. If a specific item or term is important to a transaction in goods, you must write it in the contract. Specific requirements of the parties written into agreements still control over the relaxed Article 2 rules. Finally, the drafters of the code tried to promote fair dealing and high standards of behavior in the marketplace. There are specific Article 2 sections about the duty of all contracting parties to act in good faith. The code also recognizes the concept of an unconscionable contract, or one that is grossly unfair or one-sided. The code gives the courts powers to remedy such unfairness. The code also imposes certain standards of quality on sellers of goods by providing implied warranties on goods. Warranties will be discussed further in chapter 12.

Review of Contract Damages

The legal remedy of damages is designed to compensate the nonbreaching party and put them in approximately the same position they would have been in if no breach had occurred.

This means that when a contract is breached, the general rule is to compensate the party for the losses that he suffered because of the breach. Compensatory damages usually include such things as the cost of procuring substitute performance, lost profits, and incidental expenses because of the breach. Consequential damages, or losses that arise as a consequence of the breach, may also be applied if the breaching party knew of your specific needs, and there are additional losses that flow from the breach. Punitive damages, or amounts to punish the wrongdoer, are not usually awarded in contract cases; those are limited to tort claims.

For example, I want a particular color of pink geranium for my front porch. It is hard to find. Last year, Green Garden had some perfect Light Pink Americana geraniums, so this spring I went in the shop and reserved and paid for eight plants at $3.50 per plant. Now it is May and I am ready to fill the flower box. However, Green Garden did not receive a shipment of Light Pink Americana this year. All they have is Dark Pink Americana which really won't do at all. I am owed damages to put me in the same position I would be in if no breach had occurred. In other words, I am owed my $28.00 back. Before I ordered, I didn't have any pink geraniums and now I don't have any pink geraniums. I am compensated for the deal. I cannot claim extra expenses because they promised to try to get them. I cannot claim emotional distress because my front yard is less inviting. Twenty-eight dollars will take care of it.

Contract Damages in Sales Transactions

Let's face it, businesspeople are out to make a buck. As much as everyone wants to honor their promises, it isn't always economically or commercially feasible. In the fall of 1996, if I would have had a contract to ship my 500 Tickle Me Elmo dolls to Toys "R" Us for $10 a doll, I would have been despondent. Those dolls went for upward of $2,000 a piece in the Christmas frenzy. Even if I could have gotten only an average of $1,000 per doll (in other words, if I would've breached that contract), I could have walked away with almost half a million dollars. In that situation, I would have wanted to know what could happen to me if I breached my agreement with Toys "R" Us.

Tickle Me Elmo may be an extreme example, but there are good business reasons to breach contracts all the time. The UCC in Article 2 provides clear guidelines for the consequences of doing so, and it recognizes that on occasion it makes good economic sense to break a deal. Also, with the fast-moving nature of goods and commerce, Article 2 recognizes that sometimes a merchant cannot perform on a promise because the goods are not available, despite a good faith effort to provide them. The code explains how damages in this situation should be handled.

The basic rule of compensatory damages is applicable in contracts for sales of goods, but sometimes, you may need to figure out what really compensates a business for a loss.

To illustrate, let's assume The Lady's Shop orders 50 of the latest neon-colored watches from Time of Your Life, Inc., for $100 per watch to be delivered on April 10. That date comes and goes, and no watches arrive. For three days the owner, Eve, attempts to confirm the order and shipment. Finally Eve spends three more days and $60 in long distance phone calls trying to find an alternate supplier. She locates 50 neon-colored watches at Moments, Inc., for $130 each. She has saved $50 in shipping, however, because Time of Your Life, Inc., was requiring Eve to pay this and Moments, Inc., included it with the order. What will compensate Eve for her loss? She expected to pay $100 per watch times 50 watches, or $5,000 plus $50 shipping, for a total of $5,050. She did pay $130 per watch times 50 watches, or $6,500. The difference is $1,450. She also spent $60 on phone calls and lost one week's worth of sales.

Is Eve entitled to nothing because she didn't pay any money down, or is she entitled to $1,450? You could argue that she should get nothing because before she placed the order, she had no watches, and after she placed the order, she had no watches. However, if this were the rule between merchants, how could any business ever rely on buying or selling their products until the deal was done? This would really put the brakes on business. Also, sales of goods, especially sales of goods between merchants, can have wider consequences. In this case, Eve ordered other merchandise for her store to go with this accessory. She lost over one week in sales time to procure alternate product. Her budget for this department of her shop is affecting her ability to order shoes. And what about the $60 phone bill? What if Eve did not try to find replacement goods? Could she sue the supplier for the $5,000 original contract amount?

When the seller breaches the contract, compensatory damages are figured by the *market price* that the buyer must pay to cover the missing product, less the contract price that was agreed upon. In this case, the market price of the replacements was $6,500, and this is $1,450 different than the contract price with Time of Your Life, Inc. In addition, there was $60 spent on phone bills, which were directly incurred because of this breach of contract and should be added to Eve's damages, for a total of $1,510. Eve should not get a windfall of $5,000, which is the original contract amount. This measure of damages is punitive, and no seller would ever commit to fill orders unless he had the goods in hand, with this potential liability hanging over his head. The lost week of sales is something that Eve will have to absorb as a cost of doing business. Who can tell if any watches would have sold in that time or not?

Thus, when a seller breaches a contract for the sale of goods under Article 2 of the UCC, the measure of damages is the cost to cover the breach. Why would a seller fail to perform his contract? It could be because he cannot provide the goods he promised through no fault of his own, such as shipping delays of component parts.

It is harsh to hold a seller responsible for damages if he did all he could, but remember, he will probably be receiving compensation for the breach of contract he suffered, and he was free to refrain from contracting until he had the goods in his hands if he wanted to be extra safe. Sellers take risks to keep commerce moving, and they price accordingly.

The other reason a seller would breach a contract is that the contract price is no longer good for the seller. In a fast-changing market, a commitment made a month ago may be a loser. If neon watches now sell for $170 per watch, Time of Your Life, Inc., could get $8,500 for this order today. It would be worth breaching this contract with Eve if you could make $3,500 more in gross profit, or $1,990 in net profit (after you pay Eve's damages and her phone bill).

Article 2 does not let a jilted buyer sit back and get unjustly enriched. The nonbreaching party to a contract has a duty to mitigate his damages. This means he must try to reduce or lessen the damages by taking steps to prevent the loss by getting replacement products for a slightly higher price or using a less expensive but compatible component part. Eve can't mitigate the breach by buying watches for $500 a piece. This is not reasonable, and *mitigation* must be reasonable. If it is impossible to mitigate the loss with replacement goods, contract damages would be figured on the contract price. In this case, since Eve paid no down payment for the merchandise, her damages would be limited to the $60 expense she incurred because of the contract breach. If she had made a deposit or paid for the watches, she would be entitled to a return of her consideration given.

What if the tables were turned in The Lady's Shop situation? What if, after ordering the neon watches, Eve changes her mind and calls Time of Your Life, Inc., on April 6 and cancels her order? Time of Your Life, Inc., now has to mitigate its damages by trying to resell the product. If they can resell the watches for more than $100 apiece, they will be happy and keep the bonus they made due to Eve's breach. If they can resell the watches for $100 apiece, they will come out even. If they sell the watches for less, they will have lost profit. If the merchandise sells for $75 apiece, the damages necessary to compensate Time of Your Life, Inc., are $25 per watch times 50 watches, or $1,250. Why would a buyer breach a contract for which they are liable for $1,250 in damages? One reason could be that they no longer need the materials. Perhaps the matching neon outfits are on back order, or perhaps fashion has changed. It could be cheaper to pay damages than spend $5,000 on merchandise that you know will not sell. Perhaps the price of neon watches has gone down significantly, such that Eve can now get 50 comparable watches for $20 apiece. She could breach her contract with Time of Your Life, Inc., spend $1,000 for the same amount of merchandise, pay $1,250 in damages, and still spend $2,750 less. Again, one could argue that there are no damages for Time of Your Life, Inc., because before the cancellation they had 50 watches and after the cancellation they had 50 watches, but this approach would allow buyers to cancel their contracts for no good reason.

On occasion, goods are so special that they are essentially of no use to anyone but the contract parties. In that instance, specific performance is a remedy that is available to the injured party. *Specific performance* is the equitable request to a court to order the exact performance of the contract because damages will not suffice. If I special ordered a unique Volkswagen Beetle with a pink polka dot exterior and blue fur interior, I'm probably stuck with it.

THE LAW IN ACTION

Rose is in the flower business now. She is a merchant, and she is ordering from her wholesale distributor. Contracting rules can be relaxed for the sale of goods between merchants, and this is a good example of how that may occur. Rather than stand on the formality of sending an acceptance to Rose's offer to purchase, the wholesaler sends a shipping receipt. This cuts to the chase. The contract is a done deal and the merchandise is on the way. Rather than detailing the price on each order, the wholesaler indicates "market" price, which is the reasonable wholesale rate for the flowers that day. Whatever that price is, and Rose will know from the invoice that accompanies the order, she will charge the customer accordingly to maintain her profit margin. If it is the market rate, customers will not think Rose's prices are out of line. Her merchandise is well on its way and will be available in plenty of time for the St. Patty's Day celebrations.

If this casualness makes Rose nervous, she can still request a formal acceptance and confirmation of the day's prices before any orders are placed. You always have the right to ask for specifics that are important to you in contracting, but it may slow you down a bit.

TEST YOURSELF

1. Jane was graduating from Millikin University. She arranged to lease a storage unit in Self-Store for $50 per month to keep her college items in Decatur, Illinois, until she found a job. She paid a deposit of $100 and was set to move her items into storage space H-3 on June 1. However, on May 25, Jane got a job offer in St. Louis. She wouldn't be needing the storage after all and had to cancel the arrangement. How does Article 2 of the UCC handle this contract breach and the damages?

2. Nick has contracted with Ed to buy a set of 12 antique lion figurines for $600. Nick had loved lions his whole life and he had never seen a collection like this; it contained the exact figurines he needed to complete his 100-piece set.

    Two days before Nick expected delivery, Ed called to say that he had been offered $1,000 for the pieces and Nick would have to match it or lose out. What can Nick do?

3. Pat has always been good at spotting trends. Last winter her leather goods company made huge purses studded with nail heads and adorned with chains. She had a modest contract with Saks Fifth Avenue to provide 1,500 purses for spring at $100 each. Saks prepaid Pat for the order. Saks planned to retail the purses for $200 each.

    By March, every major department store was ordering big purses from Pat faster than she could make them. Today, she could wholesale those 1,500 purses for $250 each. If Pat cancelled the Saks order and resold the purses for $250 each, what damages would she have to pay Saks in the event that they could not get alternative goods to cover the breach? What would you advise Pat to do?

Question Future Chapters Will Answer

4. Mr. and Mrs. Roth had their taxes prepared by Sam Goodyear this year. He charged them $300 for their state and federal returns. The Roths just got a notice that they underpaid their state taxes by $200 and now owe that amount and a penalty and interest amounting to another $55. Does Article 2 give them any recourse against Sam Goodyear?

Answers can be found on pages 223–224.

KEY POINTS TO REMEMBER

- Contracts between merchants, or those in the business of buying and selling products, must move quickly.

- The Uniform Commercial Code is a compilation of rules about contracting that was designed to promote uniform and predictable agreements.

- The UCC is not law, but it has been adopted, in some version, by each state in the United States.

- Article 2 of the UCC provides rules about the sale of goods.

- Article 2 rules ease the statutory and common law contract rules to allow more flexibility in contracting.

- Article 2 allows for contracts to include open terms, to be accepted by shipment, to be accepted with different terms, and to be accepted with modified terms.

- Contracting parties are always free to require exact terms in their deals.

- Contract damages are meant to compensate the nonbreaching parties for the benefits of their bargain.

- If a buyer breaches a sales contract, damages are the lost profits to the seller.

- If a seller breaches a sales contract, damages are the cost to cover, which is the market price for replacement goods less the contract price.

- The nonbreaching party to a contract has a duty to try to mitigate or minimize his damages by seeking alternate goods or reselling the goods, thereby lessening the damages owed by the breaching party.

- If damages are not adequate to compensate the nonbreaching party because the goods are unique or a special order, specific performance may be available to force the breaching party to perform the bargain.

Warranty Contracts and Products Liability

Oh, for the old days, when everyone lived in Mayberry, USA. If your car needed work, you went to Gomer Pyle. He fixed everything. You didn't go to Goodyear for tires, and Midas for mufflers, and Ziebart for rustproofing. If you had a complaint about your haircut, Floyd would gladly fix it. If you needed a fact from the county clerk, you went to Howard Sprague and got a personal, although windy, answer. No voice mail there.

Our world doesn't operate the way Mayberry did. Many of today's purchases come with warranties that include pamphlets of information in microscopic print and the return postcard to verify the date and place of purchase along with your age and income information. Is the warranty effective if you don't return all that stuff? How do you know who to go to if the product isn't right? We are hearing about so many more products liability lawsuits against manufacturers that it seems that protections for the consumer take effect only after some damage is done. It isn't like the old days, so this chapter will update you on warranties in today's market and the current state of products liability litigation.

IN THE REAL WORLD

In 2005, a diner at a Wendy's restaurant found a section of a human finger in her bowl of chili. The patron spit out the digit, reported the incident to the management, and got sick to her stomach. Did Wendy's breach a warranty to the customer? Is it an express or implied warranty? Does the patron have any claims other than the one for her money back? Was she injured in any way so that a products liability claim based on negligence may apply? Is Wendy's liable if they can prove they get all the ingredients from other manufacturers and that every employee on duty had "all 10 fingertips" at the time of the incident? Does Wendy's have any defense it can assert to avoid liability?

KEY CONCEPTS

A *warranty* is a guarantee given by one of the contracting parties that makes some promise about the item being sold. Often in the bargaining phase of contracting, a seller may "talk up" the item to be sold. A warranty is not a representation or a sales pitch that comes before the bargain is struck. A warranty is a written promise that becomes material to the bargain. The promise becomes part of the consideration that the buyer is relying on when making the deal. Sellers offer warranties because buyers who are spending money on the product want assurances that the seller will stand behind the product if it does not perform as promised.

Not every contract situation involves a warranty. To attach to the contract, the promise has to be in writing and has to be given at the time of the purchase. If the written agreement is silent on the subject, it is likely no warranty applies. Sometimes sellers specifically indicate that there are no guarantees about the contract and sell an item *as is*. This means the buyer better look closely because he is taking the item with all its faults.

The Relationship Between Warranties and Products Liability

If a warranty is involved in a contract, what the buyer gets is a promise that the seller will indemnify the buyer if the facts warranted prove untrue. To *indemnify* means to make good any loss or damage that occurs. It is different from a promise to pay compensatory damages. If a stove warranted against pilot light failure causes a gas leak and explosion because the pilot light malfunctions, the warranty promises to make the pilot light right with a repair, replacement, or maybe refund of purchase price. It does not promise to pay for a new kitchen because of the ensuing explosion. A warranty provides a contract remedy to indemnify, or make right.

Often a breach of warranty results from a malfunctioning product. Such a product often causes an accident or injury with personal and property damages. So, the breach of warranty begets a tort claim. The tort claims that result from malfunctioning items are called *products liability claims* because they involve products that have caused liability for the seller, manufacturer, or distributor.

Types of Warranties

There are three types of warranties you are likely to come across: *express*, *extended*, and *implied*. Let's look at these in more detail.

Express Warranty. Just as the name implies, this is a warranty created by words—written words. It could be offered to guarantee the proper performance of the item for a period of time. It could be offered to assure the buyer that his "satisfaction is guaranteed." The fact that a warranty applies to an item may make a buyer feel more confident about the reliability or longevity of the seller's business. The fact that a warranty is offered could ease the pain of shelling out a lot of money for an item. They can be offered for a year, a number of years, or the life of the product. Warranties for the life of the company may seem like a good deal, but depending on the condition of the company, that term may be very short. Warranties for the life of the product are usually for the usual life of a usual product. Grandma cannot take that apple corer back to the hardware store 50 years later and expect a replacement.

Since a warranty is a term offered by a seller, the seller is free to give whatever protection he wishes. Therefore, it is important to read the exact terms of the warranty. The seller may require that you return an item to a manufacturer instead of the seller. The seller may exclude some aspects of repair from the warranty; it may warrant parts, for example, but not labor to fix an item. This type of protection is sometimes called a *limited warranty*. In addition, a seller may require you to use the product as directed, or the warranty will not apply. And finally, a seller could make a warranty nontransferable or applicable only to personal, not business, use of the item. Warranties are available to read before a purchase and are often posted online at product websites.

Unless the warranty is nontransferable, it attaches to the product, not the person buying it. So it is not necessary to return the postcard with demographic information to make the warranty applicable. These cards can help you and the company determine when an item was purchased, but a sales receipt does the same thing. It is assumed that most items in commerce today will have multiple users. Others drive my car, a neighbor sometimes uses our lawn mower, and on occasion, my son even throws his own load of laundry into the washer and dryer.

Extended Warranty. An *extended warranty* is really not a warranty at all. It is a *service contract*. If a seller offers a limited-time warranty on a product, say one year, he may also offer an extended warranty that would provide additional coverage on repair costs beyond that time. This additional warranty is sold, usually at the time of the original purchase. However, it is not a warranty or a promise that is part of the original consideration for the deal; it is extra consideration paid for an additional promise. It may cost less than obtaining the service from another if the product needs repair, and it may give the purchaser a certain peace of mind, but it is a service contract, nevertheless.

Implied Warranty. An *implied warranty* is one that arises by operation of law. This means the warranty is imposed by a law, rather than by a written promise from the seller. Because society wishes to protect purchasers, who rely on the claims of sellers, federal and state laws have been passed to require basic fitness in the marketplace. In addition, the UCC, in Article 2, which deals with sales of goods, imposes minimum guarantees on sales transactions. An implied warranty promises that the product is merchantable—that is, that it is fit for the ordinary purposes for which it is used. So, my hair dryer should be fit to dry hair, my lamp fit to light my room, and my fan fit to cool my house. I should not expect wires hanging out of the hair dryer or a loose socket in the lamp or open blades whirling around on the fan. This implied warranty of merchantability can also protect the seller because it also means that I should not assume my hair dryer is appropriate to steam the wallpaper off my kitchen. A product should be fit for what it is intended for, and if it is misused, perhaps the seller is not liable for damages that result.

Article 2 of the UCC, in section 2-314, sets forth some tests for merchantability in addition to fitness for the purpose for which the product is sold. These conditions of merchantability include the following:

1. Goods should conform to any promises or statements of fact made on the container label.
2. Goods should be adequately packed and labeled.
3. Goods should be of the same kind, quality, and quantity within each unit.
4. Fungible goods, such as grain or coal, should be of average quality for the kind of goods described in the contract.
5. Goods should conform closely enough to the description in the contract to be acceptable to others in the trade or business.

The law also recognizes that consumers these days may not be as knowledgeable about products, since there are so many of them, as the sellers or retailers. Sometimes I think I know what product I need, but I am not sure.

Not long ago, I wanted to repaint my bathroom ceiling. I know that bathrooms need durable paint because of the moisture and I know that there are some products that claim to retard or prevent mildew stains.

Off I go to the hardware store. I stand in the paint department and ask a 17-year-old boy about bathroom paint. He points me to a product "perfect" for my job—mildew-resistant, stain-resistant, semigloss, low-odor paint. I tell him that my bathroom ceiling has a small crack in the plaster and I want the paint to cover that up so it doesn't show through. He tells me this is "just the thing." I buy a gallon. In this situation, an implied warranty, of fitness for a particular purpose, has been created.

Whenever a buyer asks a seller or manufacturer for advice or counsel about a product, such that the seller knows the particular purpose the item will be used for, and if the seller gives specific advice about product choice based on the particulars, a special implied warranty is created. It is more than just a guarantee that the product is fit; it is an assurance that this product will meet your specific requirements. This warranty can be created by a 17-year-old boy on the sales floor with a comment such as "just the thing." This warranty is effective against the retailer and the manufacturer, so in effect, manufacturers should know who is selling their products in the market and what they are saying about them, because the salespeople could be binding the manufacturer to warranties. Therefore, manufacturer's representatives visit retail sites regularly to see how their products are displayed and to educate the sales staff on the correct uses of the items.

The UCC grants another implied warranty that protects buyers. This is the implied *warranty of title*, which means that in a sale of goods, the seller implicitly warrants or guarantees to the buyer that he has good title and ownership to the item being sold and that the goods are free and clear of any claim by another. Therefore, buyers can be confident that upon giving their consideration in a contract, they will get an item as their own.

Products Liability Claims

Products liability claims are related to warranties. As we saw in chapter 6, the law imposes liability on parties for negligence. In a sales transaction, if an item does not perform as promised or expected, negligence could be involved, in that the manufacturer or seller could have breached a duty to the consumer and caused damages. Perhaps someone was not as careful as he should have been. The baby carrier manufacturer should have done more tests to discover that the carrier tilts at a dangerous angle when removed from a car. The bike helmet manufacturer should have known that the chinstrap would snap on impact, causing the helmet to fly off. The soup manufacturer should have checked other batches of tomato soup made the same day to know that too much salt was added to batch C-12. By definition, these "should have known better" situations result in unfit products. However, warranty claims usually just replace or repair the malfunction; they do not handle the consequences of defective product.

Therefore, the law allows victims of unfit products to pursue tort claims to recover their damages from faulty goods. Products liability claims are based on three types of situations: defective manufacture, defective design, and failure to warn. Products liability claimants do not need to prove privity of contract. *Privity of contract* means there is a relationship between the parties to a contract. We mentioned in chapter 10 that I have no right to butt into my sister's contract with her beautician, even if she did get a lousy haircut. The parties to a contract are the ones who have rights to enforce, not any other interested party. But products liability claims are based on negligence, not the contractual relationship, so anyone injured by a product may sue, even if he or she were not the original party to the purchasing contract.

Defective Manufacture. A products liability claim based on *defective manufacture* is basically the claim that the buyer got a "lemon." Sure, most printers of this make and model work just fine, but mine is a bummer. It is always getting a paper jam, makes terrible grinding noises, and is extremely slow to start a job. The particulars claim that it prints 33 pages per minute, but I've never seen that happen. I've had my computer geek friend to my house two times, so I know I didn't goof up the installation. Still, I lose connection with the network all the time. I got a dud and the manufacturer or seller should replace it. Unfortunately, defective manufacture can apply to items more serious and dangerous than my printer. Tainted food is one example, and the damages can go far beyond replacing a can of soup. Defective manufacture of an automobile can cause deaths and significant property damage. To avoid claims of defective manufacture, sellers should keep production standards high and inspection vigilant.

As in other damage situations, the buyer or user has a duty to mitigate damages, so if you know the brakes on your car are not dependable, perhaps you should refrain from using it until you get it inspected. However, this mitigation might involve other costs—a rental car in this instance—so damages can be incurred in these situations. The law makes the party who should have known, or at least should have been in a better position to identify the problem, take the bulk of the liability. I'm just an occasional consumer; the manufacturer deals with this product every day. It should take the brunt of the liability for malfunctioning items.

Defective Design. A products liability case based on *defective design* is holding up the whole of the product as faulty. A manufacturer does not have to design an absolutely safe product. For example, table saws have to be sharp. However, if the design of an item is unreasonably dangerous, such that it will cause damages to the public as made, it should be taken off the market or redesigned. For example, a table saw without a blade guard could be unreasonably dangerous to distribute to the public. The manufacturer knows that accidents will happen and the manufacturer also knows that the small added expense of a blade guard could avoid most of the risk. The law requires that a manufacturer design products free of unreasonable risk to protect the buyers who are not as knowledgeable from great harm. Often poorly designed products do make it to the market, only to reveal some defect, such as a toy with a part children can choke on. In this instance, manufacturers usually recall the product to prevent damages cases, and the product warranty reimburses the customer for the cost of the item.

Failure to Warn. A products liability case based on *failure to warn* can occur if a product caused an injury that the manufacturer failed to warn about. There is no duty to warn against obvious dangers, such as "This product is sharp" on a paring knife's packaging. There is also no duty to warn against misuse, such as interior house paint containing a warning "Not suitable for exterior use." A suitable warning could be "Do not inhale fumes. Use outdoors or in well-ventilated area." In today's litigious society, we are seeing more and more warnings on more and more products, even about obvious situations. These are probably the outgrowth of some lawsuit or claim in the past, and manufacturers do get carried away with these labels on occasion.

Defenses to Products Liability Claims

As with other negligence claims, a manufacturer can use a number of defenses to try to avoid liability for products liability claims. One common defense is obviousness. In other words, any reasonable person should have known better than to blindly cut through that wall with a hacksaw. The victim's burns resulting from cutting through a live electrical wire were caused by his own negligence, not that of the hacksaw manufacturer.

Another common defense is *alteration,* or misuse, of the product. This defense never fails to remind me of my father, who was forever fiddling with everything. He would rig up an extension to this or add a fan to that. The words *reasonable and ordinary use* were not in his vocabulary. If you use an iron fire poker for a fly swatter, you may have holes in your walls.

Finally, a manufacturer could defend itself against liability if a case is brought too late. Statutes of limitation apply to products liability cases. While the exact time limits vary from state to state, an injured party cannot sit on his rights indefinitely. All parties deserve timely notice of an injury, the right to collect evidence before it becomes stale, and the ability to examine the product in question.

Strict Liability

As mentioned in chapter 6, the law sometimes imposes liability on a party without regard to negligence. This is called *strict liability.* The law imposes it on manufacturers and distributors of ultrahazardous or extremely dangerous products. In other words, if a child drowns in a pool of water in a rock quarry, it doesn't matter how many NO TRESPASSING signs the company hung on the high fences. The company, which deals in a dangerous trade attractive to children, will be liable. Likewise, those who deal in manufacturing explosives or keeping wild animals are liable for accidents and injuries regardless of fault.

THE LAW IN ACTION

A human finger segment in a bowl of chili is a breach of an implied warranty of fitness. Chili should be fit to eat. A breach of this warranty can cause the manufacturer of the chili to be liable, as well as the retail seller. After all, Wendy's had a duty to check its product for fitness before serving it. However, all the breach of warranty does is give the customer a refund on the bowl of chili or a replacement bowl, her choice.

Did the customer face other damages that could lead to a products liability claim? Can she assert a claim based on negligence for serving a tainted product? To prove negligence, the customer has to show a duty, breach, damages, and causation. She can certainly show duty. Wendy's has a duty to serve food fit for human consumption. She can show breach if that was indeed a human finger in her bowl. Can she show damages? Sure, this was an awful experience, but she did not go to the hospital, nor did she incur medical expenses or lost work time. She may be off chili for a while, but that is understandable. She could not have acquired HIV, hepatitis, or a virus because the finger was cooked to a safe temperature. No damages, no tort.

However, that did not stop the customer from considering a lawsuit or Wendy's from talking to her to try to settle the matter without litigation. After three weeks of investigation, it was discovered that the customer had a long history of filing lawsuits against companies. Wendy's could find no problem in the manufacture or distribution of the chili that could explain the event. The incident was affecting Wendy's bottom line. In addition to the nonexistent chili sales, Wendy's restaurants across the country were experiencing declining sales, which resulted in layoffs and reduced hours.

Further investigation revealed Wendy's had a good defense to any claim of products liability because forensic tests showed that the customer had never bitten down on the finger. It turns out she planted the finger in the chili herself. She is now serving nine years in prison for extortion, and her husband is serving more than 12 years. He got the severed finger from a coworker who had lost it in a workplace accident.

TEST YOURSELF

1. I was ready for my first car. My dad looked in the ads and found the perfect starter auto for me—a 1972 Ford subcompact called a Pinto. It had a lot of body rust, which we filled and sanded before taking it to Earl Schieb for a $29 paint job. Soon I had my bright yellow Pinto with black interior. My sister thought I looked like a bumblebee driving around town. I loved that car, even though Pintos had some problems. Apparently Ford had placed the gas tank in a position that was very vulnerable when rear-end collisions occurred. It turns out the doors weren't designed so well either. They tended to jam up in accidents. There were many instances of deadly fires. Some called the Pinto "the barbeque that seats four." Is this a warranty problem? Express or implied? Could a malfunction result in a products liability case?

2. My father-in-law, Floyd, had a window and awning business. He was working on a house and fell off his new ladder. "It just gave way," he said. He fell onto a concrete patio and broke his jaw. He had his jaw wired shut and a couple of really black eyes for weeks, but he was lucky. I was feeling he might have a warranty and products liability claim because of the ladder's malfunction. When he was able to talk about it, I learned he had put the ladder on a front stoop, like a step, and as he climbed higher, the ladder switched positions, fell off the step, and caused the fall. Does Floyd have a good warranty or products liability case? Why or why not?

3. My mother was having company visit and was sprucing up a little in the living room. She bought the product you sprinkle, like powder, onto your carpet and then vacuum up. It is supposed to make your house smell good. Mom had sprinkled, and now she was vacuuming, going backward as she did it. Whoah—the footstool! Mom fell over the stool and broke her wrist. She called me from the emergency room and said, "Ellen, I have two things to tell you. First, never vacuum backward, and second, that can should have had a warning on it saying, "Do not vacuum backward. You could fall." Is Mom right?

Brain Teaser

4. It appears that Daimler-Chrysler has struck a deal with Cerberus
    Capital Management to buy the U.S. auto division, Chrysler. I am sure
    glad I didn't just buy a Chrysler-made auto. Now all those new cars
    don't have warranties anymore. True or false?

Review and Question Future Chapters Will Answer

5. In May 2007, Purdue Pharma, L.P., the makers of OxyContin, agreed
    to a plea deal which requires them to pay nearly $20 million to
    prosecutors for false marketing. The drug OxyContin has been
    sold widely in the last six years as a painkiller that is less addictive,
    less subject to being abused by patients, and less likely to cause
    withdrawal than other prescription painkillers. In fact, the company
    knew from the beginning of its sales campaign that physician focus
    groups disagreed with this claim. Do any OxyContin customers have
    breach of warranty or products liability claims against the company?
    If the cases were not resolved with a plea, how would the government
    put the corporation in jail if it were found guilty for fraud? Would
    anyone be put in jail?

Answers can be found on pages 224–226.

KEY POINTS TO REMEMBER

- A warranty is a written guarantee given by the seller at the time of a purchase to guarantee some level of performance to the buyer.

- A warranty can be to repair or replace a malfunctioning item for any reason or under limited conditions.

- Breach of warranty claims are based on the contract and allow the nonbreaching party to the recovery that the warranty agreement provides.

- Breach of warranty claims often coincide with malfunctioning products, and damages result. Injured parties may have tort claims to bring against the manufacturer or seller based on products liability.

- An extended warranty contract is not a warranty; it is a service contract.

- The Uniform Commercial Code in Article 2 creates implied warranties on the sale of goods.

- An implied warranty of fitness for the purpose for which it is intended applies to sales of goods. This is sometimes called an *implied warranty of merchantability*.

- Warranties of fitness for a particular purpose can be created at contracting if the seller knows the buyer's specific needs.

- Products liability claims are tort claims based on negligence.

- Manufacturers of products can be negligent for defective manufacture, defective design, or failing to warn of a hazard.

- Defenses to products liability claims include obvious danger, alteration or misuse of the product, and statute of limitations.

- The doctrine of strict liability imposes liability regardless of negligence in limited circumstances.

Secured Transactions

I refer to *secured transaction*s as a *promise plus*. The *promise* relates to the underlying contract or agreement between the parties to do something—usually provide financing for an acquisition. The *plus* refers to some security, sometimes called collateral, which becomes part of the deal. A lender may need a promise plus when the borrower does not have a strong credit history, is asking for a lot of money, or is in a business with a low profit margin. In this chapter, we will analyze the requirements of promise plus agreements.

WHAT'S AHEAD

- Types of Collateral
- Attachment of Collateral
- Perfection of Your Security Interest
- Buyers in the Ordinary Course of Business

IN THE REAL WORLD

Millie, a talented and creative 52-year-old, has been sewing for years. She also knows everyone in town. Over the years she has used her sewing and embroidering skills to make children's clothes, decorate shirts for the city's bowling leagues, and provide seasonal accessories, such as eyeglass cases and quilted bags, to the local department store. She has been asked to expand her business to produce eyeglass cases and bags for 20 of their Midwest stores. This single order for over $60,000 worth of wholesale products should net Millie a profit of $26,000.

Millie wants to set up the business from her home, which already has a separate entrance, adequate space, and appropriate zoning. Her friends Jean and Sue are available to help out part-time, and her neighbor, Annette, is willing to work for her full-time. Her husband, Bob, can do her accounting, but he will need an updated spreadsheet program. Millie also knows if she gears up for this job, more business from the store is very likely, as is more word-of-mouth business from clubs, athletic leagues, and merchants around town. To really get up to speed, Millie needs to acquire more raw fabric and fasteners than ever before. In addition, she needs at least one more industrial sewing machine and one more embroidery machine. She could also use some long tables and better lighting to assemble the boxes of goods for shipment. She needs the shipping supplies, too.

Millie goes to her bank and asks for $15,000 to buy raw materials, equipment, and computer software and to cover Annette's payroll for two months. The banker wants a little more than Millie's promise to repay the loan. Does Millie have anything to offer?

KEY CONCEPTS

Contract law requires the parties to a bargain to perform on their promises. As we know and have discussed in Part II of this book, parties to a contract do not always do what they promise. In the event of a breach of contract, the nonbreaching party has the right to recover damages against the wrongdoer, but this right to recover could involve lengthy mediation or litigation before any damages are realized. For some contracting parties, this is not enough. They want the promise, plus collateral. The law of secured transactions is all about collateral, and the rules for creating security interests are found in Article 9 of the Uniform Commercial Code.

Types of Collateral

Collateral is something, usually an asset of some kind, that a contracting party has recourse to if the contract is breached.

Collateral takes many forms. It can be an item that the contracting party takes *possession* of while the promise is outstanding. For example, my brother lends me $200 until July 1, and I give him my Movado wristwatch to hold until I pay him back. My brother is holding something of value, and if I breach our agreement and do not return $200 by July 1, he could keep the watch, which is worth at least $200, or sell the watch for cash and get his money back. He does not have to sue me to get me to enforce my promise; he is holding the solution in his hands.

It could also be an asset that represents cash. For example, I have a life insurance policy that has a cash value of $800. I could give this to my brother to hold until I repay the $200. If do not pay him as agreed, he could get $200 cash value out of my life insurance policy and be in the position he would have been in if I hadn't breached my promise. Other instruments that represent cash that can be used as collateral are drafts, checks, notes, and certificates of deposit.

You can also *pledge*, or promise, some goods to repay the debt. If I had a 10-speed bike and helmet, I could pledge these goods to my brother to convince him to make me a $200 loan until July 1. He is getting more than just my promise to repay him; he is getting the legal right to take possession of my bike and helmet if I breach my promise. In a business context, goods often include items in *inventory* and raw materials.

Documents of title, like the title to my automobile, can also be collateral. If I pledged my car to my brother as collateral for my loan, I could give him the title to hold until the money is repaid. He could use the title to reduce my car to cash—that is, sell it—if I do not pay in a timely manner. In a business context, documents of title include proof of ownership, such as *bills of lading* (regarding goods in the hands of shippers), and *warehouse receipts* (regarding goods in storage).

Collateral could include accounts. If I had an account due to me from my neighbor who owes me $250 for lawn mowing on July 5, I could give that account or IOU to my brother to hold until I paid him back his $200. If I goofed up, he could go to my neighbor, present my account statement, and collect my money, thus satisfying his debt. In a business context, accounts could refer to the business's bank accounts, which take in receipts every day.

Finally, collateral could include *general intangibles*—items that represent money but are not money in and of themselves. If I had a *copyright* on a piece of music for which I was entitled to a *royalty*, I could pledge that copyright to my brother until he is repaid. The piece of paper on which the copyright is written is not worth more than any other piece of paper, but what it represents—the intangible right to receive royalties—is an asset. If I failed to pay my brother, he could collect for me and recoup his money. In a business context, general intangibles include copyrights, patents, trademarks, and goodwill.

In business, chattel paper is another asset commonly used as security. *Chattel* is an old-fashioned word for movable goods. *Chattel paper* represents someone's rights to receive money for goods from another. This usually involves consumer sales for credit. If Cindy goes to the furniture store for a new dining room set, FurnitureWorld is more than happy to sell her the goods now for a small down payment and the promise to pay off the debt over time. However, to assure that they are not just relying on Cindy's promise to repay, they take a *security interest* in the furniture. In other words, if Cindy does not pay on this purchase as agreed, FurnitureWorld may *repossess,* or retake, the collateral to satisfy the debt. Will used dining room furniture be worth enough to repay the loan? It is unlikely, but many consumers are motivated to keep their households intact, so this is a bill that Cindy will choose to pay if at all possible. The security interest is noted on chattel paper. Sometimes chattel paper is kept in electronic form, such as your Sears receipt for the stove that includes a *security agreement* in small print. Of course, this chattel paper could be pledged by FurnitureWorld to their bank as collateral for the next furniture shipment they are receiving. Then the bank has a security interest in the chattel paper and the dealer has a security interest in the dining room set. These arrangements up and down the chain of commerce keep deals moving and the economy growing.

To recap, collateral can take the following forms:

- Possession of an item of value or an asset that represents cash
- Rights to goods
- Rights to inventory
- Rights to documents of title
- Rights to accounts
- Rights to general intangibles
- Rights to chattel paper

Attachment of Collateral

Because collateralized transactions usually involve the sale of goods in excess of $500 and performance time of over one year, it would make sense to get these agreements in writing per the statute of frauds. In fact, Article 9 of the UCC requires any security agreements that don't involve possession of the collateral to be in writing. This rule is a protection for both contracting parties. The *creditor*, or the party accepting the security interest, wants a record of what he may be entitled to if the promise to repay is breached. The *debtor*, or the party giving the security interest, wants a clear record of what has been pledged and under what terms. The debtor is sometimes called the *obligor*, because he is obligated to repay money or perform some other task.

Because secured transactions involve two sets of promises, they are the kinds of deals that involve a lot of paperwork and documentation. The first set of papers, called the *note*, is the buyer's or debtor's promise to repay the amount of credit he receives. When Tom buys a house, the bank has him sign a *promissory note*, which is his promise to repay $100,000 at 5 percent interest in monthly payments amortized over the next 30 years. That promise doesn't grant the bank a security interest.

There is another document for that called a *mortgage*. When Tom signs the mortgage, he is promising that if he does not repay the promissory note as agreed, the bank may look to the collateral—which is his house—to repay the loan. The mortgage goes on to explain that the bank may foreclose against the house and sell it, keeping the money gained to apply against the loan balance. All the terms and conditions are explained in the mortgage and there are some protections for the borrower—such as notice provisions and rights to cure any default in payments—but at the end of the day, the bank could take the house out from under Tom to satisfy the promise made in the note.

In retail purchases with collateral, there are often two documents to sign also: first, a note, which is a promise to pay, and second, a security agreement, which is a statement of the rights in the collateral. On occasion, lenders combine the two documents into one, usually called a *note and security agreement*, but this document contains at least two promises—one about the debt and one about the collateral.

An agreement is said to *attach* when the creditor either takes possession of the collateral or receives a written statement in which the debtor acknowledges the creditor's rights in the collateral. In addition, the security agreement should describe the collateral in clear enough detail that the parties know what is involved; it should state the amount, payment terms, and interest rate of the debt; and it should specify that the security interest has been created as the collateral for repayment of the debt. The agreement should also describe how the creditor may be entitled to repossess the collateral upon *default*, or breach of promise. For a security interest to attach, the creditor has to give some *consideration* also. The creditor's consideration is usually the money being loaned or credit being extended.

Finally, the debtor must have some rights in the collateral—that is, he must have it available for his use. For example, Colleen buys a 2006 Prius automobile. She borrows some of the money to pay for it. She signs a note, agreeing to pay the loan back, and a security agreement giving the bank the right to the collateral if she breaks her promise. In the meantime, she gets to drive all over Missouri in the car.

In business, assets often change form. For example, raw materials become products on the shelf, or credit advanced is used to purchase inventory. For this reason, a security agreement provides that it attaches to property that the debtor may obtain in the future, called *after-acquired property*. This after-acquired property clause covers the purchase of more inventory.

That inventory is automatically pledged to the creditor, even though it did not belong to the debtor at the time of the advance. In addition, creditors often stipulate that they have a security interest in the proceeds of the collateral. Thus, when the debtor sells inventory and deposits the receipts into the business bank account, the creditor has also already attached those funds as collateral.

Perfection of Your Security Interest

In addition to attaching the security interest to the collateral, the creditor also needs to "perfect" that interest. *Attachment* protects the creditor in ensuring that the debtor acknowledges the security agreement. *Perfection* protects the creditor in assuring that everyone else in the world knows about the security agreement. Perfection is accomplished by filing a statement about the security interest publicly. Article 9 outlines how and where to file the notice—usually locally in the county where the collateral is located, but sometimes centrally with the secretary of state in the state where the collateral is located. Article 9 also outlines what the notice should contain, which has been standardized in a form used nationwide called a UCC-1. The notice, called a *financing statement*, contains the names and addresses of the debtor and creditor, a description of the collateral, the date the security interest attached, and the signature of the debtor. The notice does not need to contain the underlying information about the loan or financing. That information is detailed in the promissory note, signed by the contracting parties. Those specifics are usually kept private, and that is why most creditors use separate notes and security agreements rather than a combined form. Filings are good for five years, after which time they expire. If a secured transaction lasts longer than five years, the creditor must file a continuation statement to keep his security interest perfected.

The need to perfect a security interest underlines the nature of commerce in America. It moves fast and much of it is done on credit. If Colleen's bank did not perfect its security interest in the Prius by filing, then Colleen could decide to sell the car to Larry in Jefferson City, Missouri, when she tired of it. Larry could pay Colleen and never know that she was not entitled to sell it until the loan was paid off. The bank could be left with no collateral for Colleen's loan when she stopped making payments. The bank could possibly find Larry in Jefferson City, knock on his door, and ask for the car back, but this would also be awkward. The law needs a system to make business transactions work clearly and fairly, and that system is attachment and perfection.

With attachment, Colleen knows clearly the terms of the security agreement. With perfection, other interested parties have a place to check for existing financing statements that would put them on notice not to pay off the seller before being assured that the security interest has been satisfied. Thus, an interested buyer, like Larry, could check in the county where Colleen lives to see if a financing statement is on file for a 2006 Prius automobile with a debtor named Colleen Smith. Larry would discover who the debtor was and how to contact him to see if the underlying loan has been satisfied. If it has, the financing statement could be released. If it hasn't and part or all of Larry's purchase price would satisfy the loan, Larry should not be paying Colleen directly. He should pay the bank the amount sufficient to release the *lien* and pay Colleen the balance. If Larry finds that the amount owed the bank is in excess of what he is willing to pay, he cannot purchase the car free and clear. Larry should walk away from the deal. Of course, in automobile sales, the certificate of title is another place that security interests are noted, and many lenders actually hold auto titles until they are paid in full, so more than likely, Larry would discover the lien by looking at Colleen's car title. Not all pledged assets have certificates of title, however, so if Larry were buying Colleen's business computers, he would go through the same procedure, checking for public notice that these items had been pledged to another.

An example of perfection in a business context could involve John, who needs $10,000 to buy more component parts to manufacture his Universal Remote.

John's bank will lend him the money, but they want some collateral. John has a purchase order from Better Buy for $20,000 worth of product, due to be delivered in 30 days with payment on delivery. The bank could take a security interest in the account receivable, which is the purchase order, to collateralize the loan. John signs a promissory note and security agreement and also a UCC-1 financing statement, which the bank files with the county clerk in the county where John's business is located. John's signing of the security agreement attaches the collateral to the debt. The security interest is perfected when the UCC-1 form is filed. If John is negotiating with anyone else for credit and offers that purchase order as collateral, any interested party could check the public records and see that John is not free to pledge that asset for collateral. As long as that asset is pledged to another, John will not get additional credit against that asset, the original lender will preserve its first right to that collateral, and other potential lenders will be knowledgeable in their dealings with John.

In some transactions a creditor of consumer goods may perfect his security interest without filing a financing statement. Article 9 provides that sellers who give a *purchase money security interest* in household goods have automatically perfected their liens without filing. *Consumer goods* are defined as those used for personal, family, or household use. *Purchase money* is money advanced by the creditor to allow the consumer to buy the collateral.

Sometimes all this pledging and perfecting gets confusing. Perhaps John had already given FirstBank a security interest in some business equipment and after-acquired property. The underlying loan to FirstBank has not been paid off. Does the purchase order from Better Buy constitute after-acquired property? Perhaps it does. It depends on how FirstBank described their collateral on the financing statement. Conflicts can occur. Lenders can even agree, on occasion, to be in a secondary position to a previous lender if the asset has a lot of value to it. For the scope of this chapter, it is sufficient to recognize that lenders have an obligation to check existing records and filed information about their collateral if they engage in secured transactions. Those interested in further rules about conflicts in financing will enjoy studying Article 9 priority rules and bankruptcy rules.

Buyers in the Ordinary Course of Business

To keep commerce moving, buyers of goods have to be confident that the sellers have good title to them. After all, I don't want some area farmer knocking on my door to repossess the corn on the cob I am serving my family because Food Mart didn't pay its bill. We learned in chapter 12 that one warranty that sellers of goods imply to buyers is a warranty of good title. However, not every seller is perfectly scrupulous. At times, sellers can try to sell goods even though they don't have perfect title to them because of financing they have obtained.

According to Article 9, buyers in the ordinary course of business take goods free of a security interest given by the seller, even though the security interest is perfected. A *buyer in the ordinary course of business* is a person who buys goods in good faith from a seller who routinely deals in such goods. Therefore, when I go to the office store for some folders and copy paper, I do not have to check first with the county clerk to see if the store has given a financing statement to a creditor covering these items. I can buy in good faith and obtain good title to my purchases. Likewise, I can confidently purchase apples from the grocery store, shop for aspirin from the drugstore, and buy gas from the service station. Otherwise, commerce would be very slow and risky. Generally, the secured party is protected in this context because he knows the business probably has customers in the usual course of business. In fact, they want customers to be buying goods and generating profits for their borrowers. Also, the parties holding security interests in the inventory probably also have a security interest in the proceeds of that inventory.

If you come across someone selling Rolex watches out of the trunk of his car, you probably cannot buy that item in good faith. If you have reason to believe that an item could be stolen or not owned outright by the seller, you do not gain good title to it. Buying out of car trunks is not buying in the ordinary course of business.

THE LAW IN ACTION

Millie's banker will give her a loan for $15,000, but he wants a promise plus collateral. Millie has a number of assets to consider offering for collateral. She has some existing equipment—her sewing and embroidery machines. She will acquire additional equipment with the loan proceeds that could also serve as collateral. She will also have office equipment such as tables, lighting, and computer software that could serve as collateral. She will have raw materials on hand that could be pledged. She will be turning these raw materials into inventory that can also serve as collateral. In addition, she has a large purchase order and could pledge that account receivable. As the goods she sells are reduced to cash, the bank could take a security interest in after-acquired property or proceeds to further protect repayment of the loan.

To document its security interest appropriately, the bank will have Millie sign a promissory note, agreeing to repay the $15,000 on a certain schedule. She will also be asked to sign a security agreement that lists exactly what assets she is pledging as collateral for this loan. That security agreement is the instrument whereby the collateral is attached. The bank will also ask Millie to sign a UCC-1 form, which it will file to perfect their security interest and give notice to everyone else in the world of its position in relation to this collateral. When Millie pays the loan off, the bank will release the financing statement that is public record. If Millie does not pay her loan as agreed, the bank will have recourse to the assets she has pledged to pay off the loan. The bank will repossess the collateral and sell it for cash to apply to the loan balance.

TEST YOURSELF

1. On September 1, Tony takes his drum set to A-1 Pawn Shop and pawns it for $150. The shop owner keeps the drums and gives Tony a receipt with his money saying that he can reclaim the drums for $170 until October 1. After that date, Tony cannot redeem his drums and the shop owner is free to sell them to someone else. Is this a secured transaction? How can the debtor attach the security agreement?

2. Lily had a business meeting out of town. While driving home, she drove through Port Byron, which is a small town about 20 miles from her home. She passed a garage sale that had nice-looking furniture in the yard. She stopped and discovered a great dining room table, four chairs, and a dresser that her daughter could use this fall when she headed to college. Lily got the lot for $200 and loaded it into her pickup truck on the spot. Three weeks later, a man in a suit was at her door. He identified himself as Mr. Black from Port Byron Bank. He said the bank had a security interest in the furniture she bought at that garage sale. Is Mr. Black correct? Why or why not?

3. Both Michael and Kathy Ivers need new cars. They go to their bank and get one loan for $50,000. With that money, they buy two 2007 Honda vehicles—one Accord sedan and one Element. The plan is to pay this loan off in six years. Can the bank take one security interest in two cars? Will the security interest last for six years?

Brain Teaser

4. Suzy likes to get her Christmas shopping done early. In October, she goes around looking for all the gifts she needs for her large family and because she does not have the money to purchase all the presents in October, she puts many items on *layaway* at local stores. To do this, she makes a small deposit on the items, the store puts the items aside, holding them for Suzy, and she has 30 to 60 days to come in and pay the balance of the purchase price and get the items. There is usually a service charge of about $5 for the layaway, which is nonrefundable. Does this transaction involve a security agreement? Why or why not?

Answers can be found on pages 226–228.

KEY POINTS TO REMEMBER

- Secured transactions are contracts involving collateral.
- Collateral can be obtained by possession of the item being pledged to satisfy the debt.
- Collateral can be obtained by a pledge of an interest in goods, inventory, documents of title, accounts, general intangibles, or chattel paper.
- Secured transactions involve two promises—one to pay the underlying debt and one to give rights in some collateral to the creditor.
- A creditor must attach his security interest to the collateral. Attachment is accomplished when a written agreement clearly describing the terms and collateral is signed by the debtor.
- A creditor must perfect his security interest to the collateral to give notice to the public that the asset is pledged. Perfection is accomplished when a financing statement is filed in the public records clearly noting the security pledged to the creditor.
- A creditor who takes possession of the collateral has attached it and has automatically perfected it.
- A creditor who gives the purchase money to procure consumer goods used for personal, family, or household use has automatically attached and perfected his security interest.
- A buyer in the ordinary course of business, who obtains an item in good faith for value, takes the item free from any security interest given to another by the seller.

PART

TRENDS IN BUSINESS

In this final section, we will look at some of the trends in business for the next decade and beyond. Challenges for future entrepreneurs will come from many sources, but we will examine the effect *e-commerce* has had on business in the last 20 years and highlight some remaining challenges to the development of clear cyber-contracting rules. We will also examine the place of patents, copyrights, trademarks, and trade secrets in today's business world. At the start of the 21st century, the value of the world's intellectual property was greater than the value of all the physical property on earth. This trend will just continue. The final trend we will review is the global revolution. Included will be some basics that business practitioners should know about this shrinking world and how to succeed in it.

E-Commerce

My dad was a ham radio operator. This hobby involved having a corner of the basement rigged up with his equipment, which consisted of large metal boxes that held wires and tubes that glowed funny colors. His control panel had as many switches as a command center in a 1950's sci-fi movie. He used a semiautomatic "bug key" to send Morse code messages to hams throughout the world. When he was really sending out strong signals, the black-and-white television set in the living room would get all fuzzy, and my mom would worry that the neighbors might also be getting the interference. In our backyard was a gigantic ham radio tower with a revolving antenna on top. We moved a lot for his engineering jobs and he always chose the house we would live in based on the same criterion—he needed the highest elevation in town for his tower.

In those days, only hams were making regular contact with people in other parts of the world. Things are different now. Last year, my son, Nick, was doing a semester of study in London. When I wanted to talk to him, I used my cell phone or sent him an instant message. Obviously, these changes in communication have implications for business. What does e-commerce have in store for Nick's future?

WHAT'S AHEAD

| • Entering into E-Contracts | • Enforcing E-Contracts |

IN THE REAL WORLD

Marie makes Maine blueberry jam. She sells it in her father's shop in downtown Kennebunkport, made very popular as a vacation destination because of the Bush family compound. Mona Jackson bought six jars of jam on holiday last summer and they were a big hit in her hometown of Omaha. In fact, all Mona's friends have asked if they could get some more jam online. Mona's sister has a craft and artisans' shop, and she also wants to find out how she can get some jam in stock since she is sure it will be a brisk seller. Mona calls Marie and asks her if her product is offered online. In fact, Marie has been asked this many times, so she is considering setting up an online store. What are the points Marie must consider before doing business in cyberspace?

KEY CONCEPTS

Our discussion of e-commerce will include a review of how e-contracts are made and if the contracting rules differ much from the basics we have learned and applied so far. There are some adjustments for the electronic system of contracting, but many of the common law and UCC rules can guide your way on these deals. Then, we will discuss alternatives when e-contracts are breached. The effective enforcement of breached contracts poses one of the biggest challenges for the future.

Entering into E-Contracts

Cyberspace has changed the way parties do contracting. Individuals nowadays are rarely face-to-face making bargains using mirror image language and noting important terms. It is estimated that almost 30 percent of all holiday shopping is now done online. The law still uses many common law principles to interpret contracts made online, but some of the old rules just don't fit. Internet commerce needs laws that recognize this speed and ease of contracting as well as the lack of face-to-face dealings.

We are all familiar with *shrink-wrap agreements*, which are those small print papers inside a box when you open the new computer or software. These agreements contain the terms and conditions of the product and warranties. Few, if any, consumers read these agreements. However, almost all customers plug in the computer or install the software and indicate, before they get very far, that they "accept" these terms and conditions for use by clicking the mouse. Are these *click-on agreements* binding contracts? They sound an awful lot like unconscionable agreements, with all the bargaining power on one side—the seller's—and a "take it or leave it" option. However, courts have ruled that shrink-wrap agreements and click-on agreements do form a valid contract between parties and that the terms included in the small print become part of the deal. Sellers often include language requiring contract disputes to be mediated or to be tried according to the laws of the state that the seller chooses, which is generally more liberal toward sellers.

In some cases, agreements require a signature or acknowledgement from the buyer. Today there is technology to provide an *e-signature*, usually involving some coded or encrypted keys that serve to verify the buyer's agreement to the terms. This procedure is already beginning to sound a little primitive as credit card companies work on fingerprint scanning and other imaging to identify authorized users. Although the laws regarding e-signatures are not well developed and standardized, most states recognize the validity of acknowledging an agreement online. Standardizing legislation is being proposed, but has not been passed yet. Two groups working in this area are the National Conference of Commissioners on Uniform State Laws and the American Law Institute. These organizations helped promote the Uniform Commercial Code in the 1950s.

An online entrepreneur should be familiar with UCC Article 2 rules dealing with the sale of goods. The seller should also be familiar with the recipe for a contract. Most online businesses construct their sites as offerings, not as offers to sell. An aromatherapy business offers three room sprays for which a potential buyer can make an offer to purchase. If the item chosen is not in stock, no bargain has been breached.

Once an item is chosen and acknowledged, there is generally a checkout feature noting personal information about the buyer and shipping terms. These checkout sites may be secured—that is, protected with encoding, or *encryption*—or they may be unsecured. A buyer needs to review the information that the seller provides on the website about security, shipment, and claims or complaints. In the law, parties are just as free to contract online as they are in person. If an item is important to you, set it out in the deal. With this adage in mind, a close reading of the seller's website may reveal that items are sold "as is," no returns or refunds are offered, and no information is guaranteed secured. Since online sellers do not have the luxury of meeting their buyers, they may also include statements on their websites that require buyers to acknowledge that they have reached their majority and are otherwise fit to contract.

Online sellers of goods provide an implied warranty of title according to Article 2 of the UCC. However, online sellers have been known to offer items they do not own, or do not own outright, for sale. A buyer in the ordinary course of business, even if it is business online, gets good title to an item if he buys in good faith.

Warranties can be created in online sales, so if a point is important to a buyer, he should email the seller with specific questions about the product or its application before purchasing. Specific guarantees received in a return email can serve as express warranties for specific purposes. If the seller does not respond to your inquiries, be aware that you may not have recourse in the event of a problem.

Enforcing E-Contracts: Online Dispute Resolution

We learned in chapter 2 that parties to a dispute may obtain jurisdiction, or the right to sue to enforce a claim, in the state where the plaintiff resides, the state where the defendant resides, or the place where the cause of action arose. Where does a cyberspace transaction take place? Many times an online buyer of goods has no idea where the seller is located and doesn't really care. If a company does business via the Internet in Alaska, can it be sued in Alaska even though it has no retail outlets, salespeople, or marketing efforts in the state? The law is still developing on the jurisdictional reach of the courts to businesses that exist within their borders only online. Some states have found that a selling company has made a sufficient contract with the state by virtue of the sale to require it to respond to lawsuits. Some states are still undecided on this issue, but rather look at the amount of business an individual plaintiff or defendant does in the state to determine jurisdiction on a case-by-case basis.

Because jurisdictional issues can be confusing and unsettled in Internet commerce, many contracts provide for an alternate method of dispute resolution. A separate classification of ADR known as *online dispute resolution,* or ODR, has been recognized. As you might imagine, this dispute resolution process occurs online and is often accessed through the original purchase site. Most online disputes involve auctions or e-sales of goods, and most complaints involve issues about receipt of payment or quality of the goods being transferred.

About 40 percent of online disputes involve rights over domain names. A *domain name* is the part of an Internet address that is selected and registered by the user. Over 90 percent of all domain names are registered through a private contractor, Network Solutions, Inc., known as NSI. For example, Amazon is the domain name for Amazon.com. Of course, a company named Amazon would likely want the domain name Amazon; however, any person can register any domain name. NSI usually registers a domain name to the first registrant asking for it. Some individuals and businesses have tried to profit by registering many trade names for popular companies or catchy phrases in the hopes that one day others will want to use them. When another entity tries to use someone's domain name, a dispute can arise, and often the later user has to buy the name, or license the right to use the name, from a former registering party. I could have had a hunch that Barack Obama was going to run for president in 2008. If I registered the domain name Obama08, his organization would be out of luck by the time they got around to setting up a campaign website. To use that clearly effective trade name, they would have to deal with me. However, this abuse has now been recognized, and when one tries to benefit off the goodwill or reputation of another by "name squatting," NSI has a procedure to mediate the dispute.

Some businesses choose domain names that are very similar to the names of businesses or services with a proven reputation and established trademark. For example, I could be the first to register the domain name Oprah's Opinions. To my knowledge, Oprah does not post opinions on a separate Internet site at this time, but she may want to in the future and I am squatting on her well-known name. Moreover, anyone going to my website could well believe that it is somehow associated with Oprah Winfrey, which it is not. Oprah could request mediation through NSI and undoubtedly keep me from registering and using a site that could easily be mistaken for hers.

Another organization that monitors assigned names and disputes is the Internet Corporation for Assigned Names and Numbers, referred to as ICANN. This nonprofit organization does online arbitration internationally, resolving not only domain name disputes but also some related trademark infringement disputes.

It is not only the buyer who may want to enforce an e-contract. On occasion, sellers can have very sticky issues with dissatisfied buyers. Despite a company's lack of warranties and its attempts to satisfy legitimate complaints, sellers can face unusual damages if disgruntled buyers use the power of the Internet against them. It is not unusual for disappointed buyers to threaten to complain about a seller in chat rooms and on websites that can harm the seller's reputation. Online dispute forums are often used to resolve these issues before they go too far.

Online dispute resolution providers continue to grow as online commerce grows. Many private companies offer negotiation and mediation services for online issues. One big disadvantage of online dispute resolution remains: The determinations made by these bodies still have to be enforced, and there is no specific body or group able provide the enforcement. Online rights are still developing, as are online remedies.

THE LAW IN ACTION

Marie has a nice little business going. She could make it even bigger if she created a website and sold online. Marie could register a domain name with NSI. It couldn't be Smucker's Blueberry Jam, but it could be Marie's Maine Blueberry Jam.

In setting up her website, Marie would have to consider her pricing, shipping methods, and payment methods. She should post her policies about sales on her website, if not directly on the checkout pages. Marie could use the same website to market her product as well. A recipe section could highlight various uses of the jam. A customer comment page could provide testimonials. Marie could even place a picture of herself, in an apron, holding up a jar of jam in her father's quaint store.

In entering e-commerce, however, Marie is exposing herself to claims in jurisdictions she has not even imagined. She could easily sell jam throughout the United States and Canada and even in foreign countries. This would require Marie to become familiar with food shipping requirements in other states and countries, but she probably wouldn't run into many problems since blueberries aren't endangered or dangerous in other venues. The likelihood of liability is small also, as Marie's jam contains no preservatives or additives and is packaged in heavyweight plastic jelly jars.

Marie could have some exposure to liability if she shipped large amounts of product on credit. In the event these orders were not paid, Marie might have to go out of state and start legal proceedings to collect her money, but again, she is in control of the contract. If she is smart, she will not offer large amounts of credit freely, and she can use online dispute resolution in lieu of litigation to resolve payment issues.

TEST YOURSELF

1. A local computer consulting firm doing business since 1999 has just discovered that another business is using their Delaware business corporation name, Trident Technology, as a domain name on the Internet. The local company was using the name TridentTechnologies as a domain name, but up to now, there had been no conflict or misdirected communications. Upon realizing this, the firm immediately filed to use the domain name TridentTechnology with NSI. The interloper is a New York City individual just starting a party planning service. What else should Trident Technology do in this situation?

2. Noah wished to sell his extra trombone on eBay. He listed the item, with picture and complete description. His policy stated that all sales were final and that the instrument was being sold "as is." Jeremy, a high school trombone student, saw the ad and asked his dad to obtain a money order in their name to buy the instrument. A deal was struck. Jeremy sent the money order for $150 and Noah sent the trombone to Jeremy. But the trombone pictured had a mouthpiece on it and the instrument sent did not include a mouthpiece. A more sophisticated trombone player might have known that mouthpieces are extra, but Jeremy expected to receive what he saw in the picture, which was a rather expensive collector's mouthpiece that Noah just happened to have on the instrument when he snapped the picture. Was this a good contract? What can Noah do? What can Jeremy do?

3. Ryan was an MBA student in Chicago. His apartment lease was year-round, but he always went home to Houston in the summer to work in the family business. He went to craigslist, an online forum for personal ads, housing, and jobs, and sought a summer occupant. Adam from Virginia was coming to Chicago for a summer class and needed an apartment for two months. The parties exchanged a few emails about the terms and timing. Ryan attached some pictures of the place. Could a series of emails create a binding contract between two parties from different states about real estate in a third state?

Answers can be found on pages 228–229.

KEY POINTS TO REMEMBER

- The parties to an e-contract are still in control of the terms, as with common law, so if an item is important to a party, it should be specified in the e-contract.

- The UCC rules about the sale of goods apply to e-contracts, allowing merchants to ease up on the mirror image rule and other common law contracting rules, due to the need for a fast business pace.

- Shrink-wrap agreements, which are "take it or leave it" terms for a buyer, have been enforced as valid and voluntary contracts.

- Click-on agreements to programs and websites have been enforced as valid and voluntary contracts.

- Technology allows for e-signatures to verify online documents needing authentication from a buyer or seller.

- Online sales agreements can include warranties and terms requiring mediation of disputes.

- About 60 percent of online disputes have to do with items sold online that are not delivered or paid for.

- About 40 percent of online disputes have to do with rights over domain names.

- Domain names may be registered with Network Solutions, Inc., known as NSI.

- Domain name disputes are often mediated by NSI.

- Because of the number of online disputes, many national and international mediation and arbitration businesses are available to resolve complaints.

- One of the weaknesses in online contracting is the lack of enforcement power in the agencies that resolve disputes.

- Because of the national and international magnitude of online contracting, jurisdictional issues can be difficult when a dispute arises. There is no court of cyberspace and there are no cyberspace police.

Intellectual Property

In 1995 Jo Rowling was a divorced, unemployed mother living on state benefits. In 2006 *Forbes* magazine named her the second richest female entertainer in the world, with a personal fortune of over one billion dollars. What kind of job pays one hundred million dollars a year?

The hula hoop is an idea as old as time and its use can be traced back to ancient civilizations' dance rituals. In 1958 Richard Knerr and Arthur "Spud" Melin, founders of Wham-O Company, reinvented hula hoops in plastic and sold 20 million of them for $1.98 each in six months. How can a reinvention of an old idea gross almost seven million dollars a month?

In 1986, an Indian former bank clerk started manufacturing mosquito repellent mats and selling them under the trademark JET. Ten years later, one of India's largest industrial groups was looking to enter the mosquito repellent market. They negotiated to buy the JET trademark for $6.5 million. The acquisition price was for the trademark only, and its value was so great because the founder had delivered and marketed quality products identified with the JET insignia. Do you have an idea worth millions of dollars, too?

In this chapter we will discuss the fastest growing and most lucrative area of the law—intellectual property, including trademarks, patents, copyrights, and trade secrets.

IN THE REAL WORLD

Ike was an unlikely guy to get into a patent dispute. By day, he was a talented upholsterer. On weekends, he loved to go to drag races. I'm no expert in this, because all I know I learned from Ike, but drag racing involves two cars usually racing against the clock, side by side, on the track. There is a light tower that starts the drivers off. The tower first flashes a red light on the top. Then the orange bulbs in the middle light up. Finally, the drivers get the green light at the bottom and begin the race, at which point the timer starts ticking. Races are won and lost by tenths or even hundredths of a second. Ike had a thought about a device that would help a driver with the timing situation. He saw racers trying to guess when that final green light would go on. All the lights were timed in sequence, but many drivers counted from the first red light and miscalculated the optimum time to hit the accelerator. Starting too early disqualified you for the day—an expensive mistake if it happened early in a race day—and starting too late by a second or so was deadly. The cars weren't that different in their condition and power; it really was a matter of timing.

Ike built a digital delay box that attached to the accelerator of the race car. When the driver saw the first red light, he hit the pedal. The delay box counted exactly the time until the green light and automatically engaged the accelerator at the optimum second to win the race. No more counting down. The driver needed to respond to the first light only, not the entire three, and it made a big difference. Ike could not build the boxes fast enough. Soon every driver had to have one just to be even with the others. Ike was making thousands of dollars at his hobby. He never thought of a patent. It was just fun to do. Was there any downside to Ike's proceeding in this fashion?

KEY CONCEPTS

Intellectual property is the term used to describe the intellectual and creative processes that culminate in a product—putting words or music together to sound a certain way, designing a software program to perform a certain function, or developing an item to look a particular way. The property right is memorialized on a piece of paper that does not have much intrinsic value. However, obtaining that patent, copyright, or trademark could have you on your way to a bulging bank account. Protecting these inventions and discoveries is big business and maintaining trade secrets is a current issue in the news.

Trademarks

A *trademark* is a distinctive mark or logo that is put on a product. A manufacturer puts the mark on his products to identify them as coming from him. If you go to McDonald's, you will see trademarks all over the place. Usually a trademark is identified by a TM or a TM in a circle (™), after the mark or logo being protected; a registered mark is noted by an R or an R in a circle (®). Marks can just be put into use, registered on the state level, or trademarked on the federal level for protection. The mark can be one word or a phrase. For example, at McDonald's, every time the word *McDonald's* is used, a TM appears after it. Likewise, the words *Ronald McDonald* and the golden arches logo are identified as trademarks. A McDonald's drink cup has no fewer than eight trademark notations on it.

A product is marked to identify its origin on the market. Usually, a person who uses a mark or a symbol to identify a business or product is protected in the use of that trademark. The law does not want consumers to be confused, so establishing a trademark by use or registration gives the owner of the mark exclusive rights to that mark. This is an intangible form of property. If your product is as popular as a Big Mac, that mark is a sign to any consumer worldwide. The consumer knows precisely the product he will get if he purchases a Big Mac. The mark is controlled and monitored by the owner of the mark, so some small-time burger joint in Tuscaloosa cannot call its flat, plain burger a Big Mac. It has no right to profit from McDonald's reputation or to alter that reputation by substituting its own product.

Other trademarks easily recognizable are Xerox, Microsoft, Pepsi, Nike, and Hershey's. With each of these terms, a product or company comes to mind. It represents to you a certain standard of product, a certain price range, and a certain quality. The reputation precedes the item itself by virtue of the trademark. If price is no object, consumers prefer Starbucks coffee to Folgers, a Coach leather bag to one from Payless, and a Lexus to a Saturn. Of course, part of what you are paying for in those pricier options is the protection of the image, the élan of the product.

Before 1946, people and businesses acquired trademarks by use. If you marked or identified a product or name, you gained exclusive rights to use it. Of course, there could have been an ice cream vendor in California using Freezee Pop as a name for a frozen treat and a vendor in Connecticut using Freezee Pop also. It is unlikely that vendors this far apart would run into confusion or problems. However, distribution in the United States changed dramatically after World War II. It was recognized that with more national commerce, companies that used similar marks could confuse consumers. The federal government passed the Lanham Trademark Act in 1946 to provide some national guidelines. Up to this time, vendors acquired rights to marks by use or by state registration systems, but companies expanding nationwide were concerned that their marks could be diluted or diminished in value if confused with those of another business. This was also a liability concern. Johnson & Johnson did not want to expose itself to a lawsuit because of rancid baby lotion distributed by Bud Johnson in Peoria under the name Johnson's Lotion. Therefore, protection extended not only to identical marks, but also to similar marks that could cause confusion to the public.

Trademarks began to be registered federally with the U.S. Patent and Trademark Office in Washington, D.C. To be eligible for a federal trademark, a vendor has to put the mark to use. A party cannot speculate on future marks and business names or phrases and file to protect them. Registration is renewable between the fifth and sixth year after the initial registration. Thereafter, registration can be renewed every 10 years. If you cease using the mark, you cannot renew your rights to it.

A trademark gives the holder the exclusive right to use that phrase or mark. If someone else attempts to use your mark, the owner has an action against her for trademark *infringement*, which means use without authorization. Infringers can be ordered to cease using the mark, destroy any products with the mark, and pay damages to the holder of the mark.

Not every phrase is eligible for a trademark. For example, descriptive terms, personal names, and geographic locations are not distinctive enough to qualify for exclusive use until or unless they get a secondary meaning. A secondary meaning arises from use. The king of secondary meanings is Donald Trump. He has applied for and received trademarks for The Trump Tower, The Trump Taj Mahal, and many other ventures. He filed for a trademark on the phrase "You're Fired" in February of 2004 to go along with the launch of his television series, *The Apprentice*. A determination still has not been made on this application. Applications generally take about one year to be completed, but the U.S. Patent and Trademark Office receives over 185,000 requests for trademarks each year, and at the time of Mr. Trump's application, three other competing applicants arose. These included a small Michigan business, You're Fired, Inc., which did not register the mark, but has used it for years on coffee mugs, T-shirts, boxer shorts, and tote bags. Recent developments in the television lineup may negate the need for Mr. Trump to pursue his trademark of "You're Fired."

Generic terms cannot be trademarked. In a 1999 case, AOL claimed to own the phrase "You've got mail." The court found these words had everyday, common meaning and could not be protected. Neither can words like "carpet" or "wallpaper" or phrases like "I love you." Everyone has a right to use these common words or phrases without fear of infringing on another's ownership interest.

Of course, the copyright experts today are probably the people in your company's marketing department. The creative minds that work with product names and advertising slogans need a keen knowledge of not only what the public will buy but also what is eligible for protection. Millions of dollars go into developing the campaigns that establish marks in the public's mind. Millions of dollars go into protecting marks from infringement. When a million-dollar idea comes to the marketing executive, the ensuing trademark is filed on behalf of the company that owns it. The employee, who is doing the work for hire, may get a great bonus but he does not own this intellectual property.

Service Marks and Certification Marks

A *service mark* is like a trademark, but it distinguishes the services of one company from another. The mark could be any word, name, logo, symbol or color used in commerce to identify a product. For example, the car rental agencies Hertz, Avis, Enterprise, and Budget all have marks or insignia associated with their names. Often companies use their official name or a shortened version of their official name for service marks, such as "Citibank" as the service mark for Citibank, N.A., or "Greyhound" as the service mark for "Greyhound Lines, Inc." Usually the service mark is identified by an SM after the mark being protected. Service marks can also be images like the leaping deer symbol used by Deere & Co. on its products or even colors like the distinctive Deere & Co. green. In practice, the legal protections for trademarks and service marks are the same. Like trademarks, service marks establish a recognizable image or product with the inventor, manufacturer, or distributor. A service mark such as the "LV" design on a Louis Vuitton handbag is so recognizable and so closely identified with luxury goods that inferior imitations of the product copy the "LV" mark rather than any other design detail to convince the consumer to buy.

A *certification mark* is also similar to a trademark. It may be registered to show that the vendor belongs to a group or association. The UL TESTED stamp is a certification mark of the Underwriter's Laboratory. This lab allows the use of the mark to appear on members' products that meet the testing standards of the laboratory. Having this mark on an electrical product tells a purchaser something about the quality of the item and adds value to the product. Other certification marks include the GOOD HOUSE-KEEPING SEAL or union tags.

Patents

Patents are all about inventions. A *patent* is a grant from the federal government allowing an inventor exclusive rights to his product for 20 years. This means the inventor has control of the production, use, and distribution, which can be a very valuable and lucrative right. Like an inventor, a designer can apply for a patent; a patent on a design is good for 14 years. To be patentable, an invention or a design needs to be genuine, novel, useful, and not obvious. These terms have a special legal meaning, and in the application for a patent, the inventor or designer has to describe the process he went through to develop the idea, note that the idea is not used for this purpose presently, prove that the idea has a useful application that meets a need, and explain why this application is not readily available or obvious to others.

A successful applicant will get the grant of a patent, which entitles him to mark his design or product with the word *patent* or *pat.* and include the number of the patent, if desired. Many applicants mark items distributed before a patent is granted as *patent pending* to put others on notice that this design or idea has been put in use. In the United States, patent protection is given to the first party to invent a design or product, as opposed to the first person to apply for it. Most other countries grant patents to the first to file for patent protection. The U.S. method means that disputes can arise during the patenting process from claimants alleging they put products into prior use or invented the product sooner but never put it into use. An inventor can choose not to put his product in use. He still has rights to get a patent and deal with the product exclusively for the patent period.

If a patented invention or design is used without authorization, that patent is *infringed*. A patent infringer can face the same type of damages as a trademark infringer, which includes an order to cease the infringement, destruction of all the infringing product, and monetary damages to the patent holder. Patent infringement can occur even if only part of the patented product is copied or used; not all features have to be infringed upon to have a case for damages.

If an infringer wants to continue to use the patented features of the product, he must negotiate with the patent holder for a license, or a right to use the protected invention or design for a period of time. A license can be granted by the patent holder or not, depending on his wishes.

After 20 years of exclusive rights to the invention or design, a patent expires. The patent owner can still produce and distribute the product, but competition can, too. The exclusivity period of a patent allows the creator to recoup some of the development costs, which can be extensive, and benefit from his application. However, commerce moves on, and a free market is important to our economy. After 20 years, rights must be shared with the public at large. Of course, many inventors go on to phase two or phase three of their inventions well before the patents expire. Many products invented and put into use 20 years ago are totally obsolete today.

In the pharmaceutical industry, where research and development costs are astronomical, there has been a move to extend patent life by developing a secondary use for a drug. For example, if an antidepressant's patent is expiring in three years, the manufacturer could conduct trials with the drug to see if another application is helpful. Perhaps that drug could also be used effectively as a weight-loss treatment. If a secondary use is verified, the patent holder could try to prevent or delay patent expiration (and the ensuing competition) for a number of years. This strategy to survive patent expiration has not been totally successful. Drug companies are facing patent expiration on many high-income drugs between 2005 and 2009. Upon expiration, the generic market can find it worthwhile to produce the drugs in a cost-effective manner—that is, without the worry of paying a royalty or licensing fee—and gain a huge market share of the sales.

Patents must be granted to individuals, not corporations. Art Fry and Spencer Silver—the 3M Company chemical engineers who invented Post-it Notes—own the patent. They developed the product while working for the company, so their compensation for their work for hire paid them for the invention. As is the common practice in industry research and development, the employees granted an exclusive license to 3M Company upon receiving the patent. This license, which was granted in a contract between Fry and Silver as inventors and 3M Company as the licensee in effect transferred all rights to use the patent, manufacture the product, and market it, to 3M in exchange for a modest fee. Fry and Silver remain owners of the patent, but all development potential has been granted to 3M in this contract. Licensing agreements generally last for a term of years and can be renewed. The inventors continued to work for 3M and won the company's highest honors for research, as well as many international engineering awards.

In the fashion world, Parisian designer Christian Dior was once the king of licensing. By 1948 he was licensing his name to be used in the sales of furs, stockings, and perfume. Later, you could buy Dior watches, luggage, underwear, and sheets. These agreements made the name Christian Dior recognizable worldwide. At first, the quality was maintained and it was a status symbol of sorts to have a Dior item. By 1980, however, 86 percent of Dior's sales came from goods made and sold outside France through more than 160 licensing agreements. Needless to say, the quality control suffered. A Dior item does not carry the same cachet that it once did. Thus, overzealous use of licensing can diminish a product's uniqueness and cause the owner of the product idea to lose control of its marketing, image, and quality control.

In today's fashion world, Ralph Lauren is the king of licensing. His company prefers licensing over manufacturing. Presently, Ralph Lauren provides the design and the lifestyle image, and it licenses with 350 manufacturers worldwide to create its products. The company has strict standards for production and pricing points, and it keeps a close watch on its licensees. If you buy a Ralph Lauren item, you know what you will get and you get what you expect.

Copyright

Copyrights are all about expression. The Copyright Act of 1976 protects original work that falls into the following categories: literary works; musical works; dramatic works; pantomimes and choreographic works; pictorial, graphic, and sculptural works; films and other audiovisual works; and sound recordings. Software has been added to the types of expression that can be protected by the Computer Software Copyright Act of 1980. To be protected, the work must be in a medium that can be perceived, reproduced, or communicated. It is not possible to copyright an idea; only an application of an idea can be protected.

A *copyright* is a grant by the federal government to the creator of a literary or artistic production of the exclusive right to the property for the life of the author plus 70 years. For copyrights owned by publishing houses, the protection is for 95 years from the first date of publication or 120 years from the date of creation, whichever is first. Thus, copyrights have a longer initial life than either trademarks or patents. However, you are not required to register with the U.S. Copyright Office in Washington, D.C., to get protection of your work. This is because the United States and 162 other countries subscribe to the Berne Convention of 1886 and its amendments, which provide for international copyright protection for works published after March 1, 1989. Also, a copyright owner does not need to place a copyright symbol on his work. While some works include a C in a circle (©), the abbreviation *copr.*, or the word *copyright* on the work, such symbols are unnecessary. In today's world, if you create it, you own it.

Copyrights, like trademarks and patents, can be infringed if an unauthorized person uses all or part of the original item. Infringers can be ordered to cease using the protected material, destroy all copies, and pay damages based on the harm caused or the amount of damages provided in the Copyright Act, which is not to exceed $150,000. An infringer can also be liable to answer for a crime in addition to the civil damages owed the owner of the copyright. Copyright infringement is a form of theft for which the damages can be fines or imprisonment.

There is a *fair use* exception provided in the Copyright Act which allows persons or organizations to use copyrighted material in certain circumstances, including criticism, commentary, news reporting, teaching, scholarship, and research work. Fair use also depends on how much of the copyrighted material is used for the above purposes. Using a one-minute clip of John Wayne's image in a documentary about the Wild West would probably be okay. Inserting John Wayne into a Super Bowl Sunday beer commercial is probably not. Of course, if a company were interested in that type of advertising, it could always contact John Wayne's heirs and negotiate a royalty to pay for use of the copyrighted material.

Trade Secrets

Trade secrets are just as valuable to a business as a patent or a trademark, but they are not meant for public consumption. A *trade secret* is information or a process that gives a company a competitive advantage, and that advantage is meant to be protected.

Trade secrets include the recipe for Kentucky Fried Chicken and the formula for Coca-Cola. It could be a customer list and pricing information. If I were competing for a government contract, I would love to know how my chief rival can price his products so low. If I were working for *Vogue* magazine, I wouldn't want the Easter cover idea to be known to *Harper's Bazaar*.

Trade secret protection often depends on the diligent efforts of the company trying to keep the secret. Companies use protected software, divide sensitive formulas among key employees, and use confidentiality agreements with stiff monetary penalties for breach. Once a secret is disclosed, it is almost impossible to staunch the damages. The consequences for a company can be grave.

However, if anyone out there has the recipe for that filling in an Oreo cookie, feel free to pass it along to me.

THE LAW IN ACTION

Ike came up with an idea of how to beat the clock. An idea is not patentable, but an application is. His application was to invent a product that took the "human error factor" out of the timing. To his surprise, his side venture generated a lot of interest and a lot of money. He was selling digital delay boxes all over the country. In fact, he was sharing design tips with his friends at the track and some buddies were re-engineering Ike's boxes into fancier units. Ike did not take steps to protect his invention for his exclusive use, but it was a hobby and he was making *lots* of money.

Patents are not like copyrights. You can claim a copyright just by writing something down. No other steps are required. With inventions, however, if you put it out there in the market and don't protect it, others can take your idea. How many of us have had hula hoop–sized ideas, but never did anything with them? Sometimes, if you snooze, you lose.

Over a period of the next two to three years, Ike's digital delay box improved to sleeker models and more accurate timers. From time to time, other small vendors appeared and disappeared with their versions of the device, but they never made it as big as Ike. Then one day Ike got a notice from a Mr. Samuels, a Californian claiming to be the inventor of the device warning Ike to cease and desist from selling the item due to his pending patent of the device. The notice also demanded royalties or licensing revenue from Ike for all the boxes he had sold as an infringer.

Luckily for Ike, the patent had not yet been issued to Mr. Samuels. Ike stepped into the patenting process to prove that he was the prior inventor of the digital delay box. To prove this, Ike needed to round up some of the original boxes, dig through his pile of old schematics, get some drag racing buddies to make out sworn statements, and come up with any other evidence he had. The ensuing battle had high risks and high rewards. If Mr. Samuels won, Ike would owe thousands and thousands of dollars in royalties to him and be put out of business. Samuels would get the patent and basically own the industry because his disposition was to challenge any competitor out of existence.

If Ike won, he still would not get the patent granted to him. For one thing, it was not his patent application. For another, putting his invention into popular use without protection for years had made it no longer unique. The idea was in the public domain. But a win for Ike would mean that Samuels would not get Ike's big bank account, nor would he put Ike out of business in the future. With these high stakes, the parties settled the issue. Ike did not contest the patent and did not pay damages. He was granted a relatively cheap license on his future production of his invention. Mr. Samuels continued his march to patent approval. But both parties spent thousands of dollars in legal fees to resolve this matter.

TEST YOURSELF

1. Martha and Gary Minor of Heath, Ohio, want to start a small video store. They wish to use the name MGM Videos, Inc. Will this be a problem? Why or why not?

2. Joya Williams worked as a secretary to Coca-Cola's global brand director. She stole confidential documents and samples of products from the company and in May 2006 offered them to the "highest bidder." One company receiving the offering letter was Pepsi, which warned Coca-Cola. What should Coca-Cola do? Should Ms. Williams be concerned?

3. Lauren writes music and performs it with guitar accompaniment. She is only in college, but she is a natural at putting together haunting words and melodies. She has scored her music using her computer software. She has laid down some tracks using her computer's recording capability. She has even had a work performed by her high school choir. Does Lauren hold the copyright to these creations?

Brain Teaser

4. In February 2005, three twentysomething guys started a video-sharing site called YouTube. The contents of the site come from subscribers uploading movie clips, blogs, and original videos for others to enjoy. Anyone can watch most videos, but subscribers have unlimited access and can also upload an unlimited number of items. The idea caught on like a California wildfire.

    In October 2006, Google, Inc., announced it was acquiring You-Tube for $1.65 billion dollars. As part of the acquisition, Google also became the proud owner of a number of copyright infringement lawsuits filed against YouTube because users uploaded copyrighted material without permission. Should Google be liable for copyright infringement? Should Google be liable for uploads that link to copyrighted materials?

    In a related matter, Google is now facing a domain name claim from Universal Tube & Rollform Equipment Corporation out of Ohio. The manufacturer purchased the domain name Utube in 1996. In August 2006, the company received 63 million hits on its website due to the confusion between its domain name and YouTube. The legal action about rightful claim to the domain name is still pending. Who do you think should win?

Answers can be found on pages 229–231.

KEY POINTS TO REMEMBER

- Intellectual property is the fastest growing area of property rights worldwide.

- Intellectual property includes trademarks, patents, copyrights, and trade secrets.

- Intellectual property is an intangible property right, as the paper containing the grant of rights is not valuable in and of itself, but it represents a design, invention, or creative work that can generate value.

- A trademark is a distinctive mark or logo put on a product.

- Trademark protection is granted by the U.S. Patent and Trademark Office and is good for as long as the owner puts it to use and renews its registration periodically.

- Trademarks are used to avoid confusion among consumers and create value for business.

- Descriptive terms, geographic locations, personal names, and generic terms are not eligible for trademark protection.

- Service marks are used to distinguish the services offered by one company from another.

- Certification marks from a group or association verify the vendor's item as meeting a standard set by the certifier.

- Patents are granted on inventions for 20 years and designs for 14 years.

- A patent gives the owner exclusive rights to the item protected, including the right to manufacture, distribute, sell, and license the product, or do nothing to promote it.

- Using a patented invention or design without authorization is called infringement and courts can award patent holders significant damages due from the infringer.

- A copyright is protection granted a created work such as literature, music, drama, video, or sculpture to give the creator a period of time to control use and distribution of his work.

- It is not necessary to file for copyright protection for a work; but rather, reducing it to a form that can be communicated to others is sufficient to protect the work.

- Copyright infringement is the use of protected creative work of another without permission.

- Copyright laws have fair use provisions allowing use of parts of creative works for scholarly and news-related circumstances.

- Trade secrets include information about a business that gives it a competitive edge.

- Trade secrets include formulas, recipes, marketing plans, customer lists, and pricing.

Global Business and International Law

Last year, family friends in Iowa hosted a foreign exchange student from Germany. Hans was a very bright 16-year-old attending high school and associating with others his age. In Berlin, Hans enjoyed drinking wine with his family and in public. He was quite put out that he could not enjoy alcohol as freely in the United States. After all, he is not an American and he has been drinking responsibly for years. What law should apply?

We've all heard the adage "When in Rome, do as the Romans do." In this global age, it is more important than ever to know just what the Romans do, and the French, the Japanese, the Chinese, and the Germans. Hans's complaint will not precipitate an international incident, but even a small social custom can be problematic in a foreign setting. Hans has to follow the drinking laws in Iowa. His host family cannot slip him a bottle of wine for his room as a courteous gesture without risking a call from Children and Family Services. When the host family's son, Alex, is an exchange student in Germany next year, the flip side of this issue will be in play.

Like this personal example, it is important in business to recognize cultural differences and be prepared to deal with them. In this chapter we will discuss some of the similarities between global business practices and some differences. We will also look at the trends and issues to watch in the near future.

WHAT'S AHEAD

- The Principles of Comity and Sovereign Immunity
- Doing Business Internationally
- International Payment
- Ethics and International Business
- Intellectual Property Issues in Global Commerce
- Understanding Cultural Differences

IN THE REAL WORLD

In recent years, Jack Canfield has become a highly successful author. With Mark Victor Hansen, Mr. Canfield wrote the *Chicken Soup* book series, which offers homespun advice, and inspirational stories in over 105 titles, including such specialties as *Chicken Soup for the Christian Soul*, *Chicken Soup for the NASCAR Soul*, and *Chicken Soup for the Preteen Soul*. Their books have sold over 100 million copies and are available in 54 languages. One untapped market is China, which has the potential to make 100 million books look like a drop in the bucket. Are there any contract or intellectual property issues to work out before going into this market? Are there any *Chicken Soup* titles that should be avoided in this market due to cultural differences?

KEY CONCEPTS

Just as each state in the United States has the ability to make its own laws that apply within the state, each country on the planet has the ability and authority to govern those within its boundaries. On some issues, countries have joined to find common ground, and various countries have formed alliances or agreements for those purposes. The North American Free Trade Agreement is one example of countries agreeing on terms of trade and tariffs between them. The European Union is now an alliance of 27 member states that use a common currency, a single market, and a common trade policy. Many countries agree to work together on particular issues, and those agreements are memorialized in treaties between countries or alliances for purposes such as nonproliferation of nuclear weapons, environmental protection, and disease research and treatment.

The Principles of Comity and Sovereign Immunity

At the heart of international transactions is comity. *Comity* is the principle that each country should give effect to the laws and court decisions of another country. Comity is based on respect between nations and diplomatic courtesy. Although the United States does not have a monarchy, it respects diplomatic channels and deals appropriately with the sitting monarchs of foreign countries. When President Bush welcomed Queen Elizabeth II to the United States, he afforded her all the courtesy and respect a foreign leader expects, including a state dinner at the White House. For her part, Queen Elizabeth II has welcomed every United States president since Dwight D. Eisenhower with the same pomp and circumstance, regardless of each executive's individual political affiliations.

Related to the idea of comity is the principle of *sovereign immunity*. Every country is sovereign, or independent. This idea protects nations and their dignitaries from having to answer to and appear in foreign courts. Foreign embassies located in the United States are not part of the United States, but small islands of a foreign country. Likewise, a U.S. embassy abroad is essentially American soil in that country. Foreign diplomats working in the United States have diplomatic immunity, which protects them from having to be subject to American court jurisdiction. This does not mean that all embassy employees can do as they please in the United States. The protection of sovereign immunity applies only to activity carried on in the United States by the foreign nation. Failure to pay for a personal speeding ticket can still land a diplomat in trouble.

Doing Business Internationally

It can be very attractive to manufacture or distribute products for sale globally. Decreased production costs and shipping costs make it possible to pursue distant markets more profitably than ever before. The attractively low production costs in some foreign countries have proven irresistible to American companies in the last decade. Not only is labor cheaper abroad, but foreign venues often have less regulation involving environmental issues related to production. On the flip side, foreign nations see benefits in locating in the United States. For example, Japan has found that manufacturing certain automobiles in America is a good way to fill growing orders quickly and respond to warranty and postmanufacturing issues efficiently.

Selling your product to buyers in other countries involves exporting. Companies can directly export their goods to overseas purchasers or sell their goods through an agent or foreign representative. Either way, going global involves complex contracts and requires an understanding of foreign laws to avoid costly mistakes. Large firms in major cities practice international law, and often they have branches of their firms in the foreign location to assist businesses with shipping, distribution, and tax issues.

Many companies choose not to set up their own businesses abroad but rather to license the right to another entity to conduct a particular business in a foreign place. In some countries, the law requires all or some business owners to be citizens of that country or to have investments or assets located there. This requirement can be met if businesses franchise, or contract, with foreign interests to run the business abroad. McDonald's is a fixture in almost every country in the world by virtue of granting licenses and franchise agreements to others.

These complex business deals are almost always reduced to writing. However, there are unique issues with foreign contracts. For example, one issue that may arise very soon in negotiation is the language to be used for the contract. Not every U.S. contract term has an equivalent in Thailand, for example, so choice of language is critical. Next, there is a decision to be made on laws that will apply in the case of a dispute. The choice to interpret a bargain according to French law or English law could make all the difference to the parties. These issues need to be reviewed with appropriate counsel so the parties can make informed decisions. International mediation of disputes is available, and if those resources are to be used, this fact should be specified in the contracts and clearly agreed to by all parties. Of course, in today's world, these writings often consist of faxes or electronic communications sent between the parties rather than one document formally signed by each party in one location at the same time.

International Payment

Electronic banking makes payment between international merchants easy and fast. It also makes these payments vulnerable to online theft and fraud. Another issue with international trade is the currency exchange rates that apply to the transactions. To accomplish its banking efficiently, an international business most likely will deal with a commercial bank with correspondent or associated banks in foreign countries. Competing on the global stage involves making choices in banking arrangements. International banking is a very specialized field and businesses need professional advice on this issue. It is not only individuals who get unbelievable emails touting large foreign lottery winnings. Unwary businesses have found themselves involved in money laundering schemes and worse by impulsively following foreign "get rich quick" investment opportunities without doing adequate homework.

Ethics and International Business

Business scandals have not been limited to the United States. Corporate greed, officer and director misconduct, and irregular accounting techniques have surfaced in most industrialized countries in recent years. Bad ethical decisions have not been limited to Enron, Arthur Anderson, and WorldCom.

One of my favorite foreign scandals is the Parmalat case from Italy. Parmalat is a dairy and food corporation founded in Parma, Italy, by Calisto Tanzi in 1961. The company expanded to be a principal European milk producer. In the late 1990s the company sought to expand into international markets and diversify by making speculative investments. At its height, Parmalat owned the Parma soccer team, a travel group, a television network, and many offshore firms. Unfortunately, many of these investments were not sound and not accurately represented on the company's balance sheet. The business was also funneling money from one wholly owned offshore firm to another. One of the offshore groups was even named Buconero, which means black hole.

Parmalat officials were not alone in this scheme. Many major banks helped fuel the problem by providing risky investment deals to build up and manage these speculative moves, not only to keep Parmalat afloat but also to make the banks' substantial investments look more solid. Unfortunately, as in the Enron situation, many of the investors in the high-risk offerings were workers and retirees who ultimately lost out completely.

The scheme came to an end in 2003 when liquidity problems began to hit hard. In total, the company had about an eight-billion-euro shortage, which is equivalent to approximately 16 billion dollars. Irregularities included intentional forgeries to "beef up" the liquidity of the business, among them a $3.95 billion account at the Bank of America that did not exist. Evidence of the account, used to finance other credit, was manufactured by company officials using a scanner, computer, scissors, and Bank of America letterhead. After this document was forged, a company official told a staffer to destroy the scanner and computer that were used in the scam.

Presently, Calisto Tanzi is in a Milan prison; his actual sentence is yet to be determined, but he has admitted to many, many financial crimes. It is estimated that before this tale is fully unraveled more than 20 company officials will be charged with crimes and possibly serve time in prison. Parmalat has struggled through a bankruptcy and has been reorganized as a much smaller business. Italy had to ask the European Union for a waiver of the EU rule forbidding state assistance to private businesses. The scandal was just too big for the Italian economy to absorb without help, since Parmalat employed over 36,000 Italians and supported the bulk of Italian dairy farms.

Ethical issues involving international business are not limited to financial dealings. Companies doing business overseas may find themselves unwittingly involved in subjects like child labor, fair trade pricing, environmental protection, and human rights. In decisions to trade abroad, the business's image and customer response can sometimes outweigh the quest for increased company profit.

Intellectual Property Issues in Global Commerce

There are some important international agreements and treaties about intellectual property protection. The Paris Convention of 1883 allows parties from one country to apply for patent and trademark protection in other member countries. The Berne Convention of 1886 and amendments thereto provide for international copyright recognition among signing countries. More recently, the Trade-Related Aspects of Intellectual Property Rights, or TRIPS, Agreement of 1994 adopts standards for international protection of intellectual property rights.

However, not every nation enforces intellectual property rights vigorously. Some businesses avoid certain foreign markets because of the danger of reverse-engineering and counterfeiting that could irreparably damage property interests. China and other Far Eastern countries engage in an active counterfeiting of goods, partly because it is cost-effective and partly because the concept of intellectual property belonging to one person or entity is not a well-established cultural principle. At times, copyrighted, patented, or trademarked items may be slightly modified, but their production is an infringement nevertheless. Popular items for copying are handbags, watches, DVDs, and videos. Pursuing infringement cases can be very time-consuming and costly. It can also be a lot like trying to hit a moving target since many operators set up shop quickly, sell a product, and move on to other items and locations.

One recent international example of the scope of intellectual property disputes involves the Zippo Manufacturing Company of Bradford, Pennsylvania. This company, started in 1936, still makes cigarette lighters in Bradford and employs only 800 people, yet the company's product is recognized worldwide and is a collector's item to many. The company holds many patents and has trademarked its unique lighter case design, with its rounded corners and edges and flip top. This small company usually spends more than $2.5 million per year to protect its trademarks worldwide. Presently four Chinese producers are alleged to be infringing Zippo's trademark and selling millions of lighters in China. An infringement case is pending in which Zippo estimates it will spend upward of $10 million to attempt to enforce its rights in China.

Understanding Cultural Differences

Success in international business endeavors involves specific knowledge of trade laws, banking regulations, and contract principles, but it also involves understanding the people you are dealing with and respecting their customs and ethics. Cross-cultural differences should not be ignored. There is a wealth of information available in sources ranging from international business etiquette guides to handbooks on meeting and greeting foreign business partners. Language schools and online materials abound with resources that make it easy for managers to travel confidently and safely abroad.

However, this aspect of international business involves an open mind as well as an open brain. One interesting study in this area was done by Dr. Geert Hofstede from the Netherlands. Between 1967 and 1973 he studied how values in the workplace are influenced by culture and summarized his findings using four primary dimensions. His insightful results are helpful for the international businessperson. For example, he finds that workers in the United States rank high on individualism. Americans are self-reliant and capable of looking out for themselves. Americans attach a low value to meeting society's obligations and appreciating cultural traditions. In contrast, Arab workers are highly rule-oriented and expect a controlled society. This attitude is due in part to the predominant Muslim faith, but it also reflects on expectations of class inequality and limited upward mobility. The populace has a low level of tolerance for uncertainty and wishes its leaders to control everything to avoid the unexpected. A low value is given to individualism, but a collective appreciation for culture and long-term commitments ranks high in value. Knowing these differences in cultural norms and expectations could help you avoid costly mistakes and miscues when doing business abroad.

THE LAW IN ACTION

I am sure Mr. Canfield and Mr. Hansen will get expert advice before they get into the Chinese market, but I am also sure that this market is too big for them to ignore. Some issues in contracting for production in China include choice of language for the contract and choice of jurisdiction in which to resolve disputes. They also must decide if the books will be produced elsewhere and exported to China. If they are, they need a distribution network. If not, they need production facilities in China. Of course, the monetary details will have to be worked out between authors, publishers, and vendors with appropriate electronic accounting and transferring of funds.

One issue the authors must review carefully is the control of their copyrighted material in the Chinese market. Material this popular can be attractive to counterfeiting. Part of the success of this series is its dependable product. These books present short, inspiring, real-life stories. If the series is diminished in quality or taste by poor translations, it will lose its appeal as a unique product. This is going to be especially hard to monitor because, to my knowledge, the authors do not speak all the various dialects used in China, although Mr. Canfield majored in Chinese history at Harvard University.

Finally, there may be some cultural considerations in choosing the titles to offer in China. The population values strong relationships, culture, and group-orientation, not rugged individualism. Perhaps *Chicken Soup for the Individualist's Soul* would not be a big seller. The country is also facing a population crisis and laws limit families to one child. *Chicken Soup for the Large Family* would also not be appropriate in this market.

TEST YOURSELF

1. A former employee of Schaeffer Manufacturing Co. of Fort Madison, Iowa, attempted to sell the company's proprietary information about fountain pen nib design to a Chinese pen company. The employee worked in engineering at the company until 2003, when he was laid off as the Fort Madison plant shut down. The Schaeffer Manufacturing Co. and BIC Corp. are engaged in a lawsuit against this former employee. Why should Schaeffer care about this matter?

2. A small Nebraska jeweler was contacted via the Internet by a French jeweler asking if the Nebraskan would be his contact in the United States for custom work the French firm provided to very exclusive

American customers. All the Nebraska dealer had to do was agree to accept payments into his local store account and then wire them out as the French jeweler directed. For his trouble, the American contact was offered 10 percent of the deposits as compensation. Are there any concerns with this arrangement?

3. Many pharmaceutical companies do not distribute their HIV/AIDS drugs to China or other Far Eastern countries because of fear of patent infringement. Patented drugs are extremely valuable assets to these companies that spent years and millions of dollars developing them. To risk their proprietary rights and rewards before recouping these legitimate development costs would be irresponsible to the company shareholders and investors.

    The Chinese government has been trying to convince the drug manufacturers to solve the problem by lowering the cost of their drugs in China. This would make the patented items unattractive to counterfeiters who could not make much of a profit on any copies. However, drug companies have not been willing to cut prices to generic levels on still-patented treatments.

    China has recently threatened to do what some other countries like Brazil and South Africa have been forced to do—go to the World Trade Organization and ask for special permission to break the patents of the pharmaceutical companies and begin producing and distributing cheap generics to save their citizens from an epidemic. What do you think is the best argument in favor of the pharmaceutical companies' position?

Answers can be found on pages 231–232.

KEY POINTS TO REMEMBER

- Countries agree to common goals and objectives through treaties.

- The principle of comity controls international dealings. Comity requires that each country should give effect to the laws and court decisions of another country.

- Sovereign immunity recognizes that each country is independent and not subject to the jurisdiction of foreign courts.

- Success in international business dealings requires contract knowledge, especially about the issue of choice of language for the contract, choice of laws, and dispute resolution.

- Success in international business dealings requires knowledge of the commercial banking system and foreign exchange policies.

- Success in international business involves understanding of foreign countries' import, export, and tax regulations as well as manufacturing and distribution process.

- International business exposes intellectual property rights to infringement that could be difficult and expensive to control.

- Success in international business requires knowledge of cultural differences, foreign customs, and ethics to avoid costly mistakes and miscues.

Acknowledgements

I would like to thank some individuals who helped make this book possible. At Kaplan University, Davenport, Iowa, my thanks go to Dr. John Neal and Dr. Michael Woods who made it possible for me to work half-time while writing this book. I would also like to thank Nancy Humes for her proofreading and comments and Velda Palos for her continuous enthusiasm and support.

At Kaplan Publishing, I must thank my great acquisitions editor, Shannon Berning, for her faith in me and her patience with a new writer. I also thank Monica Lugo, my development editor, for her encouragement and insightful questions.

I am also indebted to Justice Linda K. Neuman for her kind support and her introducing me to Tom Judge, who was a great reader and reviewer of the text.

I could not have done this project without the loving support of my son and my husband. Nick, thank you for all the suggestions and ethical insights. I rely on your counsel and respect your wisdom. Tim, this book is dedicated to you.

Test Yourself Answers

CHAPTER 1

1. Yes, Tri-State could be charged with many crimes. In fact, they were charged with over 330 counts or charges of theft by deception, almost as many counts of abuse of a corpse, and dozens of claims of making false statements on death certificates. For each body they agreed to cremate, but didn't, they could be charged with at least three criminal violations.

2. The State of Georgia through the Walker County district attorney would prosecute criminal charges on behalf of the public.

3. If found guilty of any of these crimes, which are felonies, Tri-State could be punished with time in prison.

4. Yes, the families of the deceased could bring civil charges in Walker County District Court for their damages. They could sue for breach of contract because they did not get what they paid for (proper cremation services). The families could also sue for tort damages because they have been personally injured by the pain and grief they have suffered because of the actions of Tri-State.

5. If found liable of the civil claims, Tri-State could be ordered to pay money damages to the families of the deceased for their infliction of emotional distress, pain and sorrow, and related costs.

Brain Teaser

6. Neither is easier than the other. They are just different. In the criminal case, the state has to prove its case beyond a reasonable doubt, which means the prosecution has to show that Tri-State committed these crimes and no one else. In the civil case, the families of the deceased have to prove by a preponderance of the evidence (51 percent) that they were damaged by Tri-State's actions.

Questions Future Chapters Will Answer

7. See chapter 2 for a discussion on what cases can be heard in federal court and why. This case could be eligible for federal court jurisdiction, but it was tried in the Georgia state court. Read on in the book to find out why.

8. It would be pretty hard to round up that building and put it in jail. So, how do corporations pay for their crimes? See chapter 5 for a discussion of business liability for crimes. In the Tri-State case, the owner of the corporation was held liable and is now serving a 12-year prison sentence for his criminal convictions.

9. We often hear about lawsuits involving many parties. Sometimes there are many plaintiffs, sometimes many defendants. In this case, many families banded together and sued Tri-State in one lawsuit because they all experienced the same treatment. The families also sued the funeral homes with which they had contracted for the services on the theory that the funeral homes picked Tri-State for crematory services and should have been more aware of what was going on. In chapter 2 you will find a discussion about why plaintiffs try to sue every party who may owe them damages.

CHAPTER 2

1. Yes, both Mr. Lynch and Sam have a cause of action, or case, to bring as a result of this accident and the damages it caused.

2. Mr. Lynch has a cause of action for breach of contract. He bought a heater that he thought was fit to heat his house safely. It obviously did

not work safely if kerosene could splash and cause such immediate, deadly harm. Mr. Lynch could also sue based on a tort, or personal injury claim. Four family members were killed, his son was seriously hurt, and his property was totally destroyed. Mr. Lynch could also sue for his own pain and suffering. Sam could sue in tort for the wrongful death of his family members, his own injuries, and his pain and suffering.

3. The Lynches could sue the manufacturer of the heater, Heat-all Industries, and the seller of the product, Sears. Plaintiffs want to sue every entity that could be responsible for their damages for reasons of judicial economy and apportioning damages fairly among those responsible. Remember, if the plaintiff fails to sue a party who should be present to fully hear the case, the defendant may join the party in the lawsuit by a cross-claim. Remember also, the more defendants, the more possible parties from which to recover damages.

4. The plaintiffs reside in Illinois. Heat-all Industries resides in Minnesota. Sears corporate headquarters is in Chicago, Illinois, so it certainly resides there, but it does business in every state of the union. Therefore, Sears may be sued in any state of the union.

5. Yes, this case can be filed in federal court if the Lynches sue only Heat-all Industries. There is diversity of citizenship between the plaintiffs and the defendant and there is more than $75,000 at issue for each of the plaintiffs. If the plaintiffs want to sue Sears, which resides in Illinois also, there is no diversity jurisdiction, and the case will have to be filed in the Illinois circuit court. The case could also be filed in Minnesota state court where the defendants reside. Heat-all Industries is located there and Sears does business there.

Brain Teaser

6. With these facts, the best choice is probably to file in Cook County, Illinois, and seek a state court resolution of the case. A federal court case is not automatically more important or more prestigious than a state court. You go to the place that can "speak the law" that you want to hear. One is not superior to the other.

Questions Future Chapters Will Answer

7. See chapter 5 for a discussion on the impact of where businesses reside. Chapter 14 discusses some issues involved in doing business online.

8. Even complex cases can be settled without a trial. See chapter 3 to discover other ways of negotiating a dispute to a resolution without a trial.

CHAPTER 3

Review Questions

1. Yes, the pet owners have a cause of action against the manufacturer based on a breach of contract. The manufacturer produced food that should have been fit for dogs but it clearly wasn't. The pet owners cannot sue for the tort (personal injury) to their dogs. Dogs don't have standing to sue in U.S. courts. However, the pet owners could sue in tort for their own injuries—medical expenses for ill dog, financial loss of value of pet, loss of companionship of pet, anguish, etc.

2. If Dog's Best Friend Co. does business in the 10 Midwestern and Southern states, they are subject to responding to lawsuits there. If you are in for a penny, you are in for a pound. They are willing to take profits from these states; therefore, they are bound to respond to claims against them in these states.

3. Mr. Hound is a little stingy. Mr. Hound is correct that customers who are returning dog food pursuant to the recall will expect their money back. He is mistaken about such limited damages to families who have sick pets and very mistaken about limits like this to families who have deceased pets.

Test Yourself on This Chapter

4. A settlement reached by negotiation, mediation, or arbitration would do the following:

    • Be quicker

    • Be cheaper

- Involve less publicity

- Not be an admission of guilt or liability

- Preserve customer relationships

- Preserve relationships with the dog food companies they do business with

- Show the community that they are seriously concerned and responsive

5. From Dog's Best Friend Co.'s point of view, I would want a mediator with legal experience to weigh how unintentional and unavoidable this incident was. I would want someone who would note how quickly Dog's Best Friend responded once they knew of the problem. I would also want an unemotional mediator who would question how responsive pet owners were to signs of illness in their pets and how quickly they noticed the recall and stopped using the product.

    From the pet owners' point of view, I would want a veterinarian who would know how much pain and suffering this injury caused to the pets and the owners. I would want someone who knew about dog pedigrees and breed values to correctly evaluate the damages done to the sickened animals and the value of the deceased dogs.

Brain Teaser

6. No amount of money will bring back a dead dog. Perhaps Dog's Best Friend could offer to pay expenses and the value of the animals but avoid other claims like emotional losses for the owners. Instead, they could offer to put $10,000 into a research project on kidney disease in dogs, or toward a dog shelter, or to developing safer canned dog food. This type of fair and concerned response could help Dog's Best Friend regain market trust and customer goodwill by showing concern and also promoting prevention measures.

Question Future Chapters Will Answer

7. Yes, there is a requirement that goods distributed to the public be fit for their advertised purposes. In chapter 12 we review the law of warranties in detail.

CHAPTER 4

1. Yes, capping an executive salary related to worker pay is an ethical decision. Many companies have used this technique, with different multipliers, to make a statement about the value of every worker. This is not an egoistic choice on the part of the management of Ben & Jerry's because an egoistic choice would emphasize the highest possible salary for the CEO, with the hopes that inflated levels of pay would run through all top management tiers. This could be a utilitarian choice by the company, to provide the greatest good for the greatest number, but this choice does so indirectly, by freeing funds to pay suppliers and workers fairly. This is definitely a choice by the owners to follow the principle of the categorical imperative, which operates out of pure motives. The owners are willing to live with this choice because it is a choice they are willing to have imposed on them by others.

2. Yes, receiving an executive compensation package that reflects what the market will bear is ethical. Many companies use this technique to attract the brightest and the best to lead their businesses. The willing market determines the scales paid and the benefits included. This is not necessarily a decision that respects the categorical imperative. Those who wish to outbid for talent do not generally want to be outbid themselves. This is not a utilitarian approach to compensation, offering the greatest benefits to the greatest numbers. This approach is egoistic. The company that pays top dollar wants what is best for it, and the CEO who accepts top dollar is getting what is best for him.

3. These survey results could raise legal concerns, because they could show that physicians use factors other than their best clinical judgment to treat patients. In cases where outcomes are not good, this could cause concerns about level of care and conflicts of interest. Chapter 6 on tort law discusses personal injury cases and the concept of negligence.

   These survey results can also raise ethical concerns because the statistical results indicate that physicians are being influenced by personal, egoistical concerns, such as income level and relationship to pharmaceutical companies, rather than the greatest good for the greatest number (utilitarian concerns) or the categorical imperative (pure motives).

4. Undisclosed self-interest in a loan made to another could be a crime. It is definitely against some financial aid representatives' contracts of hire. It could also be misrepresentation or fraud—principles discussed in detail in chapters 7 and 8. Ethically, this practice could be problematic. An egoist could be comfortable influencing others to choose loans that directly benefited him. This practice is not one that many believe should be universal, so it is not fostering the principles of the categorical imperative. Neither does this practice necessarily offer the greatest good to the greatest number, as there may be many better financial aid packages for students that are never presented because of the self-interest of the financial aid representative.

CHAPTER 5

1. Yes, any business that wishes to may contribute to the effort to defeat the sales tax. Businesses are guaranteed the right to free speech by the Constitution and this means that they can support any cause they wish with corporate sponsorship or contributions. Taking a side in this matter, or any other public dispute, may alienate some customers and business stakeholders, so businesses may be reluctant to disclose their politics or social views in some instances.

2. Royal Caribbean Cruise Lines could be liable for environmental violations on the state and federal level. Pollution violations are criminal charges that are punishable with large fines and possible sanctions, including corporate probation. In fact, the Royal Caribbean Cruise Lines pleaded guilty to a series of environmental violations and to date has paid over $27 million in fines. The company is also on corporate probation.

   Royal Caribbean's fines exceed the $25 million fine imposed on Exxon for the Valdez oil spill in Alaska.

3. Mr. Max would sure like to keep from incriminating himself, but he won't succeed here. The records the IRS seeks are corporate records for Max Tax Service, Inc. A business does not have the Fifth Amendment privilege against self-incrimination. Its records must be disclosed even if that disclosure might implicate others in criminal activity.

Brain Teaser

4. Nike, Inc., has every right to freedom of speech under the First Amendment. This right of a business to say where it stands on issues is political speech. No person, other business, or government entity has the right to muzzle Nike, Inc. The question that Mr. Kasky is raising is "Is this political speech?" Since the statement was made in an advertisement, Mr. Kasky argued that it is commercial speech and that when a business speaks commercially, for the purpose of selling a product, its speech should be truthful. Mr. Kasky's claim against Nike is that they were making false statements and that there is no First Amendment right to lie. If a business can always defend itself with freedom of speech claims, what is to keep it from misleading the public and misrepresenting itself with impunity? The California Supreme Court agreed with Mr. Kasky that this statement in the advertisement was commercial speech, not political speech, and that it could be challenged for accuracy. Prior to a trial on damages, Nike settled the claim by paying $1.5 million to a workers' rights group.

CHAPTER 6

1. To analyze this pratfall for its tort potential, you must first ask, who caused the hurt in this case? The ottoman, probably. Was there a duty on the part of the ottoman manufacturer to issue a warning with the sale: "Caution, this ottoman may cause people to trip and fall." Probably not, but we talk about warnings in chapter 11. Did Laura fail to replace the ottoman to its usual resting spot after vacuuming? Even if she did, it was in plain sight and it is Rob's own living room. He should know what hazards lurk there. We are weak on duty so the fact that an incident happened is not enough. Blessedly, Rob was not hurt in this fall. He lived to write comedy for years and years. No tort.

2. Does the management of a building have a duty to warn visitors that the elevator is not working? Probably yes, and in breaching that duty, by not posting a sign or locking the elevator doors or turning off the

power to the elevator, the management breached its duty. Poor Rosalind fell to her death, which settles the damages question. Was the management of the building the cause of her death? Maybe if she had not been so zealously arguing with Leland, she would have noticed the empty shaft, so perhaps the tortfeasor has a defense of contributory negligence, but not a strong one. Walking into an opening elevator might be assuming the risk that you could stumble on the door frame or get your finger caught in the closing doors. It doesn't mean you should be expecting "the last drop." All the elements are met. This is a tort on the part of the management of the building. The owners and managers they hired are liable.

3. The design of that kimono may have been a crime, but this incident is not a tort. Who is at fault? Mother Nature? There is no clear duty here, although there are horrible damages. No tort.

4. JR Ewing is sitting at his desk working late, comforted by the thought that in the last 13 episodes he has alienated every person he knew. Every family member, work colleague, and competitor has a reason to despise him. Some have good reason to fight back. But the person who opened the office door and eased in the barrel of a revolver was breaching a duty to the oil giant. Evil or not, a reasonable person doesn't expect to be shot sitting at his desk. The tortfeasor did shoot and it was clear JR was seriously wounded; therefore, damage has been done. The final element to establish is that the tortfeasor caused the damage. Clearly that person did, in a grossly negligent, if not intentional, fashion. It wasn't until the beginning of the next season that we knew the shooter was Kristin Shepard, JR's sister-in-law and mistress. Tort.

CHAPTER 7

1. David is obviously not as knowledgeable about antiques as he thought. He sold a very valuable chest for one one-thousandth of its worth. Six months ago, at the time of the sale, there was an offer and an acceptance. The parties had capacity to enter into this contract, which was legal and voluntary. The issue David really wants to raise is consideration,

but he will lose his claim. The law does not care if consideration is fair in monetary terms and will not protect people from entering into bad deals. For consideration to be valid there must be an exchange of promises or items of value—not necessarily equal value. People overpay and underpay all the time, and the law allows contracting parties to make their own deals without interference. Commerce would not be very dependable if every disgruntled seller could reclaim an item he regrets selling or if a buyer could have remorse over the price paid and return his purchases at whim.

2. The offer was the depositing of $1 into the vending machine. The acceptance was the giving of product. Consideration was present. There was no illegality or incapacity or involuntariness involved, so this was a good contract. When a party to a contract does not get what was promised, a breach has occurred. The vending machine malfunctioned, and although the coffee was not delivered as expected, the machine did perform. Judy has a breach of contract action against the vending machine company. She will probably just forget about a $1 cup of cappuccino, but if the ruined shoes were valuable, she may ask for compensation for those as a damage incidental to the malfunction. She could also consider a tort claim against the vending machine company for property damage (the shoes), and if the hot drink happened to burn her, she could make a tort claim for personal injuries. A breach of contract can easily lead to a related tort claim.

3. The offeror sets the terms. This offeror let every prospective offeree coming into the store know the conditions. Maybe Sally would like to argue that a minor is not liable for his contracts, but that won't work. Parents are responsible for their children. If Sally was concerned about Rex's ability to stand still, she should have left him at home, or at least outside the store with another adult. Sally has bought one wedding present and one smashed vase. She accepted the offer to purchase it the minute Rex flung it to the floor. Of course, some merchants don't react this way. Kids are always spilling in the grocery store aisles and the parents rarely have to pay. A jar of pickles is a lot different than a Waterford vase.

Brain Teasers

4. There's no question here that there was a binding offer and acceptance with consideration. The house has been in progress for over eight months. The parties have capacity, and it was a voluntary bargain. The only issue being questioned is legality. Is it legal for this architect, with a lapsed license, to get paid $560,000 for completing the house, or has he invalidated the contract due to the lapsed license? When it comes to legality, there is a difference between a contract being for an illegal purpose, like gambling, prostitution, or murder, and a contracting party having a technical difficulty in a license or fee issue. There is no problem with legality here. The Stars have to pay.

5. We don't know in this case who made the offer, Dan or Eric, but that doesn't matter. If Dan made the offer, he controlled the terms, and when he offered $200 for the season of snow removal, Eric accepted it. If Eric made the offer and it was not to Dan's liking, he could have counteroffered more acceptable terms. Regardless of who offered and who accepted, these parties agreed on snow removal. They set a price, which was good consideration—money in exchange for services. They are both of legal age and neither has disabilities. No one held a gun to their heads forcing them into this bargain, so it was voluntary. Snow removal is a legal subject for a contract. But is it a fair agreement? What about equity and fairness? For Dan, $100 per snow removal seems unfair. For Eric, not quite $7 per snow removal seems stingy.

    For better or worse, the law does not care about a fair agreement; the law cares about legal consideration. Dan gave up his money—either a lot of it or a little depending on the weather, but he agreed to the deal. Eric gave up his freedom, which is legal consideration. All winter, Eric had to be ready in case of storm. He could never go out of town, unless he provided backup services. He had to have his equipment in working order at all times. He was being paid as much for his availability as for his services. If either party was nervous about how the winter would turn out, they could have agreed on a per services charge for snow removal. The law will enforce the agreement made. Only Mother Nature will decide who bargained wisely.

An argument based on promissory estoppel is not available to Dan or Eric. Quasi contract and promissory estoppel are equitable remedies that the court may consider if one side to an agreement is unjustly enriched due to reliance on an agreement that does not meet the requirements of a contract. In this case, there is a binding contract. The law will interpret the agreement the parties have, not what they wished they had.

Question Future Chapters Will Answer

6.   In chapter 8 we revisit the Buyers and Sellers as we discuss whether you always have to do what you promised. This chapter will explain issues about contract performance and defenses to charges of non-performance.

CHAPTER 8

1.   Calvin and Lang Auto Body made a contract. There was an offer and acceptance, consideration, capacity, legality, and voluntariness. They exchanged promises when Calvin took the car in for the estimate. But due to circumstances, neither party performed. Calvin cannot sue Lang for failure to repair and Lang cannot sue Calvin for payment. Neither party is out anything in this arrangement so far, so there is nothing for a court to enforce. If Lang had ordered a special part, good only on Calvin's car, he may have a claim for the cost of that item. If Calvin had given Lang payment for services he never received, he may be owed a refund. It is not uncommon for parties to mean to complete their deals but fail to do so through no fault of their own. If no action has been taken, there are no damages. If Calvin does get his act together, he could set up another repair date, but depending on the terms of the estimate, Lang may claim that the commitment for that price has expired.

2.   Lou and Linda may be in love, but they are not savvy about contracts. They have been legally married by Judge Joe Brown; there is no reason to ask a court for specific performance. The purpose of the contract was for Lou and Linda to be married, not to be married by a certain

judge. In this case, one judge is as good as another. Judge Judy is not unique. They got the benefit of their bargain—which is marriage—so there are no damages.

3. Many businesses want to create strong relationships with their customers. Not only do satisfied customers come back, they also often provide invaluable advertising and promotion to others. When businesses offer "satisfaction guaranteed," they are saying that the customer has the power to rescind the bargain and the business will agree. When a bargain is rescinded, the consideration given for the deal is returned on each side of the contract. In this case, if the Browns are not satisfied with the dog, the breeder will take it back and give the Browns a refund of their purchase price. There have been incidental expenses for six months in food, grooming, and veterinary expenses, but the Browns chose to incur them before they decided if they were satisfied. It is not unusual for vendors to put a time limit on customer satisfaction, but this would depend on the item and the relationship that the business was trying to establish.

Brain Teaser

4. Parties are free to contract for any terms that are legal. Often time is of the essence in an agreement. You must have a component part by a certain date to finish the project on time. The supplies have to be here by race day. The caterer must be set up by 6:00 P.M. Timing is critical when missed deadlines mean additional setup costs, delays, or idle workers. If timing is important to contracting parties, often it is deemed to be a material element of the contract, a breach of which implies damages to be paid by the breaching party. Often the amount of damages is set out in the contract and can be substantial to mirror the material nature of the breach. At least the parties know what is important to each side and where they stand. Nine cartoons on April 15 may seem like substantial performance because it is 90 percent of what is due; however, the contract itself defines it as a material breach, so it is. Roz is out her usual $2,500 for the month plus an extra $500. It doesn't matter whether any or all of the cartoons she submitted were printed. If they were, she earned money on those. If they weren't, she felt the sting of

breaking her promise. If the April 17 offering was published, Roz still owed the $3,000 penalty for her material breach. Who knows what extra lengths and special setups *The New Yorker* staff went through to get that tardy cartoon in the next issue? That is their business. If it is used, Roz will get paid, but in the future she will probably submit 10 cartoons a month, whether she thinks they are funny or not.

CHAPTER 9

1. To determine if this agreement is a valid contract, you first must evaluate it for all the ingredients it should have. Here we have an offer, an acceptance, consideration, a legal contract purpose, capacity of the parties, and a voluntary agreement. This appears to be a good contract. Next, we must evaluate whether it must be in written form. Since this is a contract for land, it must be in writing to be enforceable. Finally, we must evaluate whether the writing is sufficient. A greasy paper napkin is not the usual place to memorialize a $60,000 deal, but it is legal. The napkin identifies the parties, the subject of the contract, a date for the contract to be performed, and it is signed by both parties.

    When Bob gets around to signing the deed over to Dan, that agreement will have to include the complete legal description of the 40 acres, but the description on the napkin is sufficient for each party to know what land they are talking about, so it is valid.

2. This is a fine contract with all the ingredients: offer, acceptance, consideration, legality, capacity, and voluntariness. Since it is for the sale of goods valued in excess of $500, it should be in writing to be enforceable, but the parties did not put this agreement in writing. That is okay in this case since no one has a problem or complaint with the deal. If Jeff or his parents were unhappy about the Buick's condition once they owned it, or if they thought that it was not operating as it should, they may have an issue with the contract. In that case, it would be hard to enforce in court because of the lack of writing, but if everything is going fine, it doesn't matter. Many people exchange property with values in excess of $500 every day with no bad consequences, but to be enforceable in court, these deals should be in writing. Incidentally, when you sell a car, you transfer a title. Generally this title includes the name

of the owner and a description of the vehicle, and to transfer it to a buyer, the seller signs his name to it, fills in the buyer's name, and usually states the price or a range the price falls within. In effect, this title is the written document memorializing the sale of a vehicle, so there was a writing after all.

3.   I have no problem with Jeff wanting to trade in the Buick, but now he is a forger and has committed fraud in his haste. If Jeff did not make the payments as scheduled on the Mustang, the bank could not collect from Jeff's parents. You are only liable on an instrument if you sign it. Jeff's parents did not sign the guarantee, so the bank cannot hold them liable. It does not matter that Jeff's parents were willing to sign the paper. Their signatures don't appear on the surety paper, so they are off the hook. It is unlikely that this would really happen however, since any self-respecting banker would require Jeff's parents to come to the bank to sign this form.

Question Future Chapters Will Answer

4.   George isn't the only student with this question. Almost everyone in the class has had part-time jobs in retail and knows that deliveries do not always match orders. How can businesses get away with this? But on the other hand, how can businesses keep up with the fast pace of commerce and always be sure they modify each purchase order or invoice with exactly matching terms? The answer is that there are special rules for merchants, or parties in the business, that allow them, in contracting with each other, to be a little more flexible in their agreements. This topic is discussed in detail in chapter 11, which covers sales contracts.

CHAPTER 10

1.   Because this is an oral contract, the parties have no document to look at that may have covered this eventuality. Instead, this contract needs to be interpreted according to state statutes and case law. There is nothing totally unique about P. J.'s painting, although it is very good. If Fritz agreed, Bruce could finish the job. P. J. would assign her obligation to finish the painting to Bruce and Bruce would assume the responsibility to complete

the job. Of course, P. J. can only assign what she has, and at this time, it is the duty to complete the job. Fritz does not have an obligation to pay Bruce or to pay more for the job than originally contracted. P. J. and Bruce would have to work out the compensation between them. Perhaps this is a trade-off for a favor P. J. did last summer; perhaps she will share some of the fee with Bruce. Of course, before he agrees to the arrangement, Fritz may want some information about Bruce's painting experience or some references from him so he can check out past painting jobs.

2.   Fritz's contract is with The Outing Club, not with Joseph. If Fritz really wanted the particular skills of Joseph, he should have contracted for them. The Outing Club kitchen is still working and the new head chef, Andrew, is very qualified. Only the original parties who have rights in a contract can enter into assignments.

3.   Buster should exercise Mom's wishes, not his own. As Mom's power of attorney, he stands in her place and should act as she would act if she were able. Mom has made her wishes known. If Buster cannot follow them due to his own convictions, he should decline to be her power of attorney, or Mom should know better and pick someone who she knows won't struggle with this type of decision.

Brain Teaser

4.   Assignment of checks is not unusual. Checks are already three-party instruments involving the *payee*, the *drawer* (check writer), and the *drawee* (check writer's bank). For JoAnn to reduce that check to cash, she has to endorse it. This is usually done by signing the back. There are many types of endorsement, including payment to a third party. To do this, JoAnn could sign the back of the check as follows:

Pay to James Smith
JoAnn Smith

Or she could sign:
Deposit to Acct. No.: [James' account number]
JoAnn Smith

CHAPTER 11

1. Leases for storage units are not covered by Article 2 of the code. In this situation, the UCC does not help at all. Article 2 only deals with sales of goods. Goods are movable items, not real estate, leases, or services. The statutes of Illinois and case law would control this case, as would the terms of the lease agreement that Jane signed. More than likely, she would get her deposit returned to her and Self-Store would rent space H-3 to someone else in June.

2. Apparently Ed made a deal with Nick before he checked around for potential buyers. Unfortunately, Ed has made his agreement and cannot now change the consideration terms just because he has a better offer. Since this is a unique collection, Nick does not have to be satisfied with compensatory damages, which would be minimal if he did not make a deposit. Nick can sue for specific performance of this contract for the sale of goods because they are rare, and damages will not adequately compensate him for the breach.

3. If Pat breached her contract with Saks and resold the 1,500 purses for $250 each, she would make $375,000, or more than double the amount she would have made if she had honored the Saks contract. Pat would owe Saks their prepayment back, which would be $150,000. Pat would also owe Saks their lost profit on the deal, which would be the difference between the retail price and the wholesale price of the purses, another $150,000, for a total of $300,000 in damages. Pat could breach this contract and pay damages to Saks and still make $75,000 more than she would if she honored the contract. Should she do it? That depends on her relationship with Saks and how they will view this breach, but it sure looks worthwhile.

Question Future Chapters Will Answer

4. To determine if Article 2 provides any recourse for the Roths, we first must examine if Article 2 applies. Mr. Goodyear provided a good (the tax returns) and a service (the labor to prepare them). Article 2 deals

only with the sale of goods, not services. But tax preparation, like many other consumer endeavors, involves a combination of goods and services. When I take my car in for an oil change, is that buying goods or services? When I go to a lawyer to get a will written, am I contracting for a good or a service?

It gets tricky. Generally, the law tries to evaluate how much of the contract involves goods and how much of it involves services. If it is about half goods, Article 2 should apply.

Mr. Goodyear did not do an adequate job of providing the goods he sold for $300. The damages that the Roths must pay total $255. It is very likely that Mr. Goodyear will have to compensate the Roths this amount for his breach of contract. The outcome, however, would really depend on the written contract, if any, between the parties and the warranties, if any, Mr. Goodyear offered on his work. Chapter 12 discusses warranties in detail.

CHAPTER 12

1. Certainly an automobile, which is a good according to Article 2 of the UCC, should have an implied warranty of merchantability or fitness to be used as an auto, not as a barbeque. The automobile also had an express warranty from Ford that the doors would function properly and that the gas tank would hold gas in reasonably predictable circumstances, including rear-end collisions. So, there were some issues of breach of implied and express warranties with this make of car.

Because bad accidents with Pintos caused so much personal injury and property damage, Ford was subject to a number of products liability lawsuits. It was discovered in investigations regarding these accidents and subsequent lawsuits that Ford knew the car had a serious design flaw but chose to ignore it. The company figured that it would be cheaper to pay off on lawsuits than to perform a relatively small and cheap redesign that could have avoided the big problem. Because Ford took such a careless attitude about consumer safety, its reputation was seriously tarnished by this model, which has been dubbed as one of the worst cars of all times. Because of this careless attitude about a known design defect, Ford was slapped with many large judgments from the litigation involving this model, including a 1981 California case involving two Pinto passengers—one who was killed and one who was severely burned. The jury awarded the burn victim $2.5 million in damages and $125 million in punitive damages, mainly because the evidence showed that Ford ignored the problem. An appellate court later reduced the punitive damage award to $3.5 million. Serious products liability cases can involve seriously punishing damages.

2. The ladder did not just "give way" as I had envisioned. Luckily, Floyd recovered just fine from this serious incident, but he did not have a warranty case to pursue. If it had failed to support his weight or if a rung had broken, it could have been a warranty case and a products liability case for the damages. And there certainly were damages in this case including a badly bruised face, broken jaw, cracked teeth, scratches and scrapes, and a few weeks off work, not to mention the medical bills. Unfortunately, the ladder company has a good defense to this accident in that Floyd misused the ladder. It came with a clear warning to use on a flat surface. This was a warning that Floyd ignored to his peril.

3. My mom is probably right about not vacuuming backward; however, she is probably wrong about the warning on the can. It is obvious that this product is going to have to be vacuumed up after use. A regular consumer is charged with knowing the furniture layout in her own living room, and the company does not have to warn against the obvious.

Brain Teaser

4. Any agreement involving a corporate acquisition must delineate how the parties are going to handle the contract obligations—including the warranties—that a party has made to third parties. Daimler-Chrysler can sell only what they have, and what they have is a combination of some assets and some liabilities. In the liabilities column are the outstanding warranties they have given to others. In the negotiation, Daimler and Cerberus will determine which party will honor these obligations and what they are worth in consideration. Although it is

unclear who will assume this responsibility at this point, new Chrysler owners will have their warranties honored.

Review and Question Future Chapters Will Answer

5. Yes, many OxyContin users may have breach of warranty claims against the company. In marketing and product information, the company knowingly included a false claim that the product was less addictive than comparable painkillers. This is at least a misrepresentation and probably fraud. Moreover, users of the drug who relied on the express warranty probably have more damages than just the cost of the drugs over the years. Addictive drugs cause many incidental and consequential damages, so these users have products liability claims against the company, including many death claims.

   The $20 million from the criminal plea agreement will go to the federal government and states and be used in law enforcement and medical programs. Since the company knowingly violated the law, its president, its top lawyer, and its chief medical officer have all pleaded guilty to criminal charges and have agreed to pay almost $635 million in additional fines. Although the company cannot be put in jail, these officials could face jail time if found guilty at trial.

CHAPTER 13

1. Tony's arrangement with the A-1 Pawn Shop is a secured transaction. Tony is the debtor and A-1 is the creditor. Tony promises to repay the debt in 30 days, plus a little interest on the money loaned. A-1 wants more than just Tony's promise, so they take possession of his collateral, the drum set. A-1 does not have to do anything else to attach or perfect its security interest because it has a possessory interest in the collateral.

   After the loan matures, if it is not paid, A-1 is holding the collateral and can reduce it to cash, or the owner can take up playing the drums.

2. Garage sales, tag sales, auctions, and estate sales are common and popular. Buyers can get great deals and sellers can unload a basement full of excess. It would not work very smoothly if every bidder at an auction had to be on the phone to the county clerk to see if that blender being held up was pledged to any secured creditor. The implied warranty of title gives the buyer confidence that the seller is free to offer the item. The fact that these buyers are generally getting consumer goods for personal, family, or household use and taking them in the ordinary course of business protects the buyers from characters like Mr. Black showing up at the door.

    Lily should advise him to go back to the bank and brush up on Article 9 of the UCC.

3. One loan or extension of credit can be collateralized with more than one item. The bank will note its lien on both vehicle titles and perfect it with public notice. A financing statement is only good for five years, so if this is a six-year loan, the bank may have to file a continuation or renewal statement after five years to keep its lien noted.

    Incidentally, if after three and a half years, the Element were no longer needed for hauling and the loan balance were down to $22,000, the Ivers could ask the bank to release the lien on that vehicle so they could trade it in on another sedan. If the bank felt secure enough in the collateral of the 2007 Honda Accord, it could just keep the lien on that one piece of collateral to secure the remaining balance. If the bank felt it needed more security, it could release the Element and ask for the title of the new auto the Ivers buy to give them enough collateral to secure the remaining balance of the original loan.

Brain Teaser

4. A layaway is not a secured transaction. There is no creditor and there is no debtor. The customer is not buying the items over time; she is holding them for an agreed upon period until she can purchase them outright. In effect, she is entering into an option contract with the store. She is getting the option to purchase the items within 30 or 60 days and for that option, she is giving consideration of $5. If she buys the items, she has exercised her option and pays the full purchase price. If

she does not exercise her option within the time period, the store has earned $5 for the trouble of holding the items, which can be placed back on the shelf for sale to another customer. Suzy needs to check with each store individually on their policy about getting her down payment on the purchases returned.

CHAPTER 14

1. Trident Technology has started to take the steps necessary to protect themselves by formally registering the name TridentTechnology as a domain name. Next, the local firm should try to identify how to contact the New York individual to send a notice to cease using the domain name because of prior use and confusion with an established business. Since an actual notice and receipt thereof is necessary in this case, an email would not be sufficient and the local firm should send a registered letter. If the interloper does not stop using the name, the local firm could resort to NSI or another online mediation service to try to resolve the issue.

    A New York party planner probably does not want to get confused with a computer consulting firm, so he should want to make an adjustment in the name he uses. In a conflict, the local firm would probably win rights to the name because it was the first to register the name and it has a history of using it.

2. Even though this was an online agreement, you can verify that it was a contract by applying the recipe. Noah's listing was an invitation to bid, not an offer. Jeremy did bid $150, which constituted an offer. Noah accepted. The consideration was the exchange of money for the instrument. The purpose of the contract was legal. It was voluntary, and the party who sent the payment, Jeremy's dad, was of legal age. There could be a bit of an issue about capacity since Jeremy struck the deal, but Noah was made aware that Jeremy's dad would be purchasing the item via his money order. Was there a mistake that could void the offer? This contract principle can apply here even though the contract was an online agreement.

There sure was a misunderstanding about the mouthpiece, and in this situation Noah's claim of "as is" works against him, because he pictured the goods with the expensive mouthpiece. Both parties were a little inexperienced in these dealings and did not clarify the terms as much as they should have.

One solution could be a mediation. Noah could provide a standard, less expensive mouthpiece to Jeremy so the trombone is useful to him. That preserves the sale and satisfies the buyer. In lieu of an agreed workout, the parties could consult the dispute resolution reference on eBay to seek mediation of this matter.

3. Ryan's and Adam's back and forth emails can constitute a contract. Adam answered Ryan's advertisement. Ryan provided pictures illustrating the subject of the contract—a 60-day lease interest in an apartment. The parties agreed on a price and effective dates of the contract.

   Promises were voluntarily exchanged between capable parties about a legal subject. This is a contract about land, so it should be in writing. This deal is in a few writings—the various emails necessary to strike a deal. Incidentally, since three states are represented in this deal, it could get sticky if Adam refused to leave the apartment at the end of his summer sublet and Ryan had to take legal action to regain his place. Would the law of Virginia, Texas, or Illinois apply? This is an easy one because most elements of the contract are in Illinois—the apartment, the holdover tenant, and the main tenant, so the Illinois courts would be the most appropriate jurisdiction to resolve any dispute.

CHAPTER 15

1. MGM is a logo and trademark associated with Metro-Goldwyn-Mayer Inc. The company started out as a movie production studio, but today is involved in videos, music, television, entertainment venues, and more. The MGM trademark, a roaring lion in a circle, is so famous that even occasional moviegoers can picture it. A business with the name MGM Videos, Inc., could easily be confused with the larger company, especially since they both deal in some of the same items. If Martha

and Gary use this name for their business, it is highly likely they will get a letter, sooner rather than later, from the legal department of the other MGM notifying them to cease and desist using the name and trademark that belongs to the company founded in 1924.

2. Coca-Cola should take steps to protect its very valuable trade secrets—including the formula for Coke. In this case, Pepsi took the ethical high ground and informed Coca-Cola of the letter they received. The FBI was called in to investigate and determined the writer was an accomplice of Ms. Williams. Not only was Ms. Williams immediately fired from her job, but she was also charged with criminal conspiracy to sell trade secrets for at least $1.5 million. This is a serious federal felony for which she was just sentenced to eight years in prison. In sentencing her, the judge noted that this is the kind of offense that cannot be tolerated in our society. Her accomplice awaits sentencing.

3. Lauren does have a copyright by use. It is not necessary to apply for official copyright protection from the U.S. Copyright Office or mark her music and recordings with a notation of copyright status. The Berne Convention gives her international copyright protection to her works if she records them in a durable medium. If there were any questions about authorship or ownership of Lauren's music, she could show the dates of her songs, which it would be wise to note on all her creative works, and prove her rights.

    Of course, if Lauren were careless about monitoring or unconcerned about the uses of her songs, she could create an opening for someone to infringe on her rights. Intellectual property rights need a lot of upkeep.

Brain Teaser

4. YouTube had a policy that stated that users could not upload copyrighted materials without permission. The system, however, was, and still is, self-policing. Unless someone with a proprietary interest in the material sees it on YouTube and complains, protected materials could be broadcast with impunity because the site has grown so large.

YouTube will shut down a site if a violation is brought to its attention, but some interested parties who could complain about a violation do not because it gives them invaluable publicity and promotion. YouTube, and now Google, have also been sued for infringement because uploaded materials contained links put in by the poster to copyrighted materials. Google was recently found not liable in a case about linking.

If timing and use determined the issue, Universal Tube & Rollform Equipment Corporation should win and get to keep the domain name Utube. YouTube should be barred from using a confusingly similar domain name. However, as a practical matter, how do you argue with 63 million hits a month? This case hasn't been decided, but it's inevitable that Utube will keep getting YouTube information, and it may be easier to modify its domain name than to sort through millions of misdirected items.

CHAPTER 16

1. Schaeffer and BIC may no longer be producing these fountain pens that have the great nibs, but that doesn't mean that the companies' trade secrets should be revealed. The companies still have a valuable asset that they may someday use or sell or license to another. You don't have to be a current employee to be guilty of breaching trade secrets. Once a secret, always a secret.

2. This Nebraska jeweler should quickly delete this email or forward it to the local office of the state attorney general to investigate. No reputable French jeweler needs a Nebraska front for transferring funds. There are commercial banks to do this quite efficiently and effectively. This deal reeks of money laundering and fraud. I doubt there is a French jeweler within 100 miles of this deal.

3. Drug companies could argue their ultimate mission—which is to make a profit. They are, after all, businesses with responsibilities to their shareholders, their employees, and their business partners. The

development of new drugs is a multimillion-dollar endeavor that is undertaken because the high investment cost occasionally yields high rewards. International business decisions are difficult because of the differing standards of living and cultural norms of societies, but businesses would choose not to develop lifesaving drugs if they had to be given away. Investors would not support these businesses, and every culture would be the worse off.

Glossary

Acquittal: A finding that a defendant in a criminal trial is not guilty.

Act of God: An event that is not caused by man, such as a flood or tornado.

Administrator: The party named by the court to oversee the affairs of a deceased who dies without a will, including the collection of assets, payment of debts, and distribution to heirs.

Advocate: A representative, one who speaks for another.

After-acquired property: Property coming to a debtor after he has given a security interest in that property to a creditor.

Alteration: A defense to a products liability case that states the product has been modified or changed in a way not suited to the item.

Alternative dispute resolution (ADR): A method of resolving a legal dispute out of court. ADR forms include negotiation, mediation, and arbitration.

Antenuptial agreement: See prenuptial agreement.

Appeal: An action taken by a party to litigation after trial to ask a higher court to review the decision.

Appellate court: The second tier of courts in the state and federal system that reviews cases that have already been tried.

Arbitration: A form of alternative dispute resolution using a neutral third party or panel to hear the evidence and render a decision on the issues. Arbitration may be binding or nonbinding on the parties to the dispute.

> **Binding arbitration:** Arbitration wherein the parties agree to abide by the decision of the arbitrator to resolve the dispute.

> **Nonbinding arbitration:** Arbitration wherein the parties do not agree to conclude the dispute with the arbitrator's recommendation.

As is: A manner in which a good may be offered for sale that indicates there are no warranties or guarantees offered on the good.

Assignee: The person in an assignment who is assigning rights.

Assignment: The transferring of rights in a contract to another party.

Assignor: The person in an assignment who is assigned rights.

Assumption: An agreement whereby a third party steps into the position of one of the original contract promisors to complete the deal. Assumptions can be with a release or without a release.

Assumption with release: Agreement to accept a third party into a contract in which the contract party assigning his rights is released from liability on the outstanding contract.

Assumption without release: Agreement to accept a third party into a contract in which the contract party remains liable on the outstanding contract and the third party is an additional party liable to perform.

Assumption of risk: A defense to a tort claim which states that the injured party knew and agreed to the risk of his actions.

Attachment: The step in a secured transaction in which the creditor gets written acknowledgement of the collateral pledged for repayment of a debt. Attachment can also occur by possession of the collateral by the creditor.

Authentication: The accepting of a writing as one's own.

Bargained-for exchange: A legal term of art used in contract law to describe the consideration requirement of a contract. The giving of value of each party to a contract.

Bench trial: A court trial in which the presiding judge renders the decision.

Beyond a reasonable doubt: The standard of proof in a criminal case which requires the judge or jury to find unanimously that the defendant performed the act that he is accused of and that no other possible explanation exists which could cause any doubt in that conclusion.

Bill of lading: A document showing an interest in goods in the hands of a shipper.

Bill of Rights: The first 10 amendments to the U.S. Constitution which were passed in 1791 to guarantee rights to private citizens. Some Bill of Rights guarantees found in the first 10 amendments:

- First: Freedom of religion, freedom of speech, freedom of the press, the right to assemble, the right to petition government for a redress of grievances
- Second: The right to keep and bear arms
- Fourth: The right to be free from unreasonable searches and seizures
- Fifth: The right to be formally charged in a capital or criminal matter, freedom from double jeopardy, the right to decline to be a witness against yourself, the right to life, liberty, and property which cannot be taken by government action without due process of law
- Sixth: The right to speedy criminal trial, the right to be informed of charges and witnesses against you, the right to confront accusers, the right to assistance of counsel
- Seventh: The right to trial by jury
- Eighth: The right to be free from excessive bail or fines, the right to be free of cruel and unusual punishment

Borrower: The person taking out a loan; the debtor.

Breach: The breaking of a promise in a contract.

Breach of contract: The failure of a party to uphold his promises.

Buyer in the ordinary course of business: A buyer of goods for value in good faith. A buyer in the ordinary course of business takes goods free and clear of any outstanding security interest.

Capacity: The legal ability to enter into a contract. To have capacity, a party needs to know what his assets are and what he wants to do with them. Impediments to capacity could be minority or a legal disability.

> **Legal disability:** A person's lack of ability—through mental impairment, illness, or injury—to know what his assets are and what he wants to do with them. A person who is aged may be under a legal disability, and therefore unable to contract legally. However, age is not an automatic disability, nor is mental impairment, low IQ, or terminal illness. Legal disability is more about mental functioning than physical abilities.

> **Minority:** In state law, being under the age of consent, usually 18, and therefore not legally capable of entering into contracts.

Categorical imperative: An ethical philosophy that finds an action ethical if it can be universalized. A believer in the categorical imperative will find an action ethical, and therefore do it, if it is an action that he is willing to have done to him.

Causation: The reason an event happens. In tort law, it is important to figure out if the person you are trying to hold liable for an injury to you in fact caused the event to happen or set a series of events in motion resulting in injury.

Certification mark: A distinctive mark granted by a group or association certifying that the marked goods meet certain standards of the organization.

Chattel paper: Chattel paper represents someone's rights to receive money for goods.

Circuits: One name used for the divisions of a court system within a state.

Click-on agreement: Contract terms that are accepted by an Internet user clicking a button.

Codes: Rules, laws. Many compiled laws are referred to as codes. For example, the U.S. Code contains all the laws passed by Congress that are currently in effect.

Collateral: An item or items of value pledged or given to a creditor to secure repayment of a loan.

Comity: Principle in international law that each country should give effect to the laws and court decisions of another country.

Commingle: To mix together, for example, a husband and wife may commingle their paychecks in one checking account.

Common law, also called case law: Previous court decisions that can be looked to for guidance on how a current matter may be resolved.

Comparative negligence: The relative fault of each party in a tort case, used to apportion damages.

Complaint: The paper that is filed to begin a lawsuit. Sometimes called a petition.

Concurrent jurisdiction: The authority of either a state court or a federal court to hear a matter.

Consent: A statement that a party knew and agreed to the possible harm of his actions, sometimes used as a defense to a tort claim.

Constituents: Parties to whom you are responsible.

Consumer clause: A clause in Article I of the U.S. Constitution stating that Congress can make laws regulating interstate commerce.

Contract: A legally enforceable agreement. A contract needs the following to be valid: offer, acceptance, consideration, capacity, legality, and voluntariness. Some common contract terms:

Bilateral contract: A promise for a promise.

Executed contract: A contract that has been fully performed.

Executory contract: A contract that is performed over time.

Express contract: An agreement formed with words or writing.

Implied contract: An agreement formed from a person's actions.

Material breach: Significant failure in performance of a contract's terms.

Oral contract: A contract that is not written.

Specific performance: An extraordinary legal remedy wherein a party is ordered to perform a contract in lieu of paying damages.

Substantial performance: Performing almost all of a contract's terms.

Third-party beneficiary contract: A contract intended to benefit a person who is not a party to the original agreement.

Unilateral contract: A promise for an act.

Valid contract: A contract that satisfies all the requirements.

Void contract: An agreement, that because of a missing requirement, may not be legally enforced.

Voidable contract: A contract that because of some defect may be terminated by one party.

Written contract: An agreement reduced to writing.

Contract damages: The amount of money that a party may recover for a breached contract. Contract damages generally give the injured party the benefit of the bargain.

Contributory negligence: The tort doctrine stating that a plaintiff who contributes to his own injuries may be barred from recovery from the defendant.

Copyright: A grant of exclusive rights to a creator of intellectual materials for a period of years.

Count: A part of a court filing that states a theory of recovery.

Counterclaim: A claim made by a party being sued against the party suing him. Courts want defendants to bring counterclaims, if they have them, against the plaintiffs so all matters between the parties may be settled in one court action. See judicial economy.

Counteroffer: The response to an offer that adds or changes the terms of the offer.

Cover: The measure of damages due a contract buyer upon breach by a seller. Cover is the market price less the contract price.

Creditor: The party making a loan.

Criminal law: The body of law that regulates public conduct.

Cross-claim: A claim made between plaintiffs to a lawsuit or defendants to a lawsuit.

Cyberlaw: Law governing transactions occurring over the Internet.

Cybersquatting: Filing for a domain name that the filer is not planning to use but is merely holding in hopes someone else will want to purchase it.

Damages: Money given to successful civil law claimants to pay them for their injuries.

    Compensatory damages: Money to compensate a party for his injuries. For example, the amount of money needed to repair a car damaged in an accident.

    Consequential damages: Money to pay expenses incurred as a consequence of the harm. For example, the amount of money needed for a rental car while repairs are made to the damaged car.

    Incidental damages: Money to pay expenses incurred as an incident of the harm. For example, the amount of money needed to tow a damaged car from the scene of the accident.

    Punitive damages: Money awarded to a successful litigant in order to punish the wrongdoer and to give him an incentive to take corrective action.

Decider of fact: The judge in a bench trial or the jury in a jury trial.

Debtor: Person taking out a loan; the borrower.

Defendant: A party being sued or accused of a crime.

Defense: A response to a claim of liability; a legal reason to absolve a party from liability in a civil or criminal case.

Deposition: A discovery device wherein a party to a lawsuit takes sworn statements from an individual for use at trial.

Discharge: A forgiveness of liability. A party can obtain a discharge by operation of law, such as a statute of limitations that bars a claim, or by a statutory grant, such as the bankruptcy law that provides for a forgiveness of debts.

Discovery: A phase of the lawsuit process in which the parties gather all the relevant evidence to be used at trial.

District: A division of the court system in a state or in the United States.

Diversity jurisdiction: The authority to take a case to federal court based on the facts that all the plaintiffs reside in different states than all the defendants and more than $75,000 is at issue.

Document of title: A paper showing the ownership of goods, such as the certificate of title to an automobile.

Domain name: The Internet address chosen by the entity—for example, westlaw is the domain name of *www.westlaw.com.*

Double jeopardy: Being tried twice for the same crime. The Fifth Amendment of the U.S. Constitution forbids the federal or state governments from exercising double jeopardy.

Draft: An order by one person to pay another through a third person; a check.

Drawee: The party on whom the check is drawn; the bank.

Drawer: The person by whom a check is drawn; the check writer; the maker of a check.

E-commerce: A business transaction that occurs in cyberspace.

Embezzlement: The fraudulent taking of the property of another.

Encryption: The coding of information online so as to make it accessible to some users.

Equity: Justice or fairness; the principle of jurisprudence that allows courts to render decisions based on justice and fairness when legal procedures are inadequate to grant relief.

E-signature: An acknowledgement of a party sent electronically.

Ethics: The study of right human behavior; moral behavior.

Exculpatory clause: A contract provision that seeks to hold a contract party harmless in advance for any negligence that may occur.

Executor: The party named in a last will and testament to oversee the affairs of a deceased including the collection of assets, payment of debts, and distribution to heirs.

Express warranty: A guarantee about the performance of a product given in writing by the seller to the buyer to induce the purchase.

Extended warranty: A contract between the buyer and seller of goods wherein the seller agrees for a prepaid fee to repair or replace goods covered for a set period of time; this is really not a warranty at all, but a service contract.

Factoring: The process of buying accounts receivable at a discount.

Fair use: An exception to copyright protection that allows use of portions of copyrighted material without permission for scholarly and news reporting purposes.

Felony: A serious crime or breach of public standards punishable by fines and prison time.

Financing statement: The form filed publicly to show a creditor's interest in a debtor's collateral.

Fraud: A purposeful untruth or concealment of a fact told to induce a party to enter an agreement.

General intangible: An item which represents money, but is not in and of itself of value, such as a patent, a copyright, a trademark, or goodwill.

Goods: Movable property other than money; merchandise. Article 2 of the UCC deals with the sale of goods.

Guarantee: An assurance given by one party to be responsible for the contract of another.

Homicide: The wrongful killing of another.

Implied warranty of merchantability: In the sale of goods, a warranty given by the seller to the buyer guaranteeing that the goods are fit to be sold and used for the purposes for which they are offered.

Implied warranty of title: A warranty involved in the sale of goods which guarantees to the buyer that the seller is free to sell the goods and that no other party has an interest in them.

Incidental beneficiary: A person or organization that may benefit from the contracts of others but is not meant to be the object of any bounty from the contracting parties.

Infringement: Using of intellectual property of another without permission. A trademark, copyright, or patent can be infringed by an unauthorized user.

Intangible property: Property that stands for something of value, such as a stock certificate, patent, copyright, or goodwill.

Intended beneficiary: A person or organization that is meant to benefit from the contract of others. For example, my husband is intended to benefit from my New York Life Insurance policy on my death.

Intentional: With the purpose of accomplishing the outcome; purposeful.

Intentional infliction of emotional distress: An intentional tort in which one party's outrageous conduct causes extreme emotional harm to another.

Internet Corporation for Assigned Names and Numbers, also ICANN: A nonprofit organization that conducts international online arbitrations resolving domain name and trademark issues.

Interrogatories: Written questions and answers between parties to a lawsuit during the discovery stage of a trial.

Inventory: Goods on hand for future sale.

Invoice: Written memorandum of an order and its cost; a bill.

Judicial duel: A medieval dispute resolution process used by aristocrats involving combat to prove truthfulness; see trial by combat.

Judicial economy: The legal principle that requires parties to a lawsuit to bring all claims they have in common in a single action to save court time and resources.

Jurisdiction: The right of a court to hear a claim and give a decision. Federal courts have jurisdiction to hear federal claims, small claims courts have jurisdiction to hear cases involving small amounts of money, traffic courts hear traffic cases.

Jury trial: A criminal or civil case that is decided by a group of the defendant's peers.

Liable: Legally obligated, responsible.

License: The right to use intellectual property owned by another. A license can be granted to a manufacturer, distributor, or seller of a good for a specific time period or for a particular geographic area.

Lien: A legal right or interest in property that a creditor gets from a borrower until a debt is satisfied.

Litigant: A party to a lawsuit.

Litigator: The attorney trying a lawsuit.

Lost profit: The measure of damages due a contract seller upon breach by a buyer. Lost profit is the contract price less the resale price.

Loveday: A medieval term for a day in which a settlement to a dispute is negotiated.

Mailbox rule: The contract rule stating that acceptances are effective upon dispatch, or when they are deposited into the mailbox, whether they are ever received or not.

Market price: The price that an item will bring at sale.

Mediation: An alternative dispute resolution process using a neutral third party to help the parties to reach an agreeable settlement.

Mediator: The neutral third party who facilitates a mediation.

Meeting of the minds: The contract process of offer and acceptance that results in an agreement.

Mirror image rule: The common law contract rule stating that the acceptance must be in exactly the same form as the offer; otherwise, it is a counteroffer.

Misdemeanor: A minor crime or infringement of the law that is punishable by a fine or loss of privilege.

Misrepresentation: A false or misleading statement.

Mission statement: A written statement of purpose for an individual or organization stating ethics, values, and goals.

Mistake: An error of fact that may serve to void an agreement. Mistakes can be unilateral (one-sided) or bilateral (two-sided).

Mitigation: Taking steps to reduce one's damages.

Money damages: Monetary award given to a successful civil litigant.

Mortgage: A document filed publicly to show a creditor's collateral interest in real estate until the repayment of a debt.

Negligence: The failure to exercise a standard of care that a reasonable person would exercise in the circumstances.

Negotiation: A form of alternative dispute resolution in which the parties to a dispute meet, with or without others, to attempt to resolve their issues by agreement.

Network Solutions, Inc., also NSI: A private contractor that registers Internet domain names.

Obligee: The party to whom a debtor is responsible; the creditor.

Obligor: A party making a promise to do something; the debtor.

Online dispute resolution, or ODR: A form of dispute resolution conducted online.

Open terms: Terms in a contract that are not specified, such as amount of product and price. Article 2 of the UCC allows contracts between merchants to contain open terms.

Pain and suffering: A type of damage claimed in tort cases to compensate the claimant for the effects of an injury.

Parol evidence rule: A contract rule that requires written contracts to contain all important terms and forbids oral testimony that modifies, adds to, or contradicts written terms.

Patent: A federal grant to an inventor or designer of exclusive rights to his product for a period of years.

Payee: The person being paid with a check.

Perfection: The step in a secured transaction in which the creditor files public notice of his interest in the debtor's collateral.

Petitioner: The person filing a lawsuit; the plaintiff.

Plaintiff: The person filing a lawsuit; the petitioner.

Pledge: To promise an item of property to a creditor as collateral for a debt.

Pleadings: Written court papers filed in a lawsuit.

Police powers: Powers granted to states to regulate matters concerning the health and general welfare of its citizens.

Possession: Having actual control of an item.

Possessory lien: An interest in a piece of collateral by virtue of having possession of it.

Power of attorney: A written document in which one party, the principal, grants authority to another, the power of attorney, to do acts on the principal's behalf.

> **Limited power of attorney:** The granting to another a limited or specific ability to act for the principal.

> **Plenary power of attorney:** The granting to another the ability to act for the principal in every capacity.

Power of attorney for health care: The granting to another the ability to act for the principal on decisions involving health care issues.

Precedent: A decided case that sets a standard or guideline for future similar cases; see also *stare decisis*.

Prenuptial agreement: A written agreement between parties to be married outlining their rights in each other's assets should the marriage fail. Also known as an antenuptial agreement.

Preponderance of the evidence: The standard of proof in a civil case. This standard requires the trier of fact, which is the judge or the jury, to find that more likely than not, the plaintiff should receive damages from the defendant; sometimes referred to as the 51 percent rule.

Principle of egoism: The ethical belief that right action is anything that benefits the individual decider.

Principle of utility: The ethical belief that right action is what creates the most good for the highest number of people.

Privilege: A special legal right granted to a person or group of persons.

Privity of contract: Mutual interests of the parties to a contract.

Procedural laws: Rules about how the court system functions, such as due dates, filing fees, and courtroom conduct.

Proceeds: What is received upon sale or disposal of collateral.

Products liability claim: A category of tort law dealing with products manufactured, distributed, or sold in commerce that do not function as promised. Claims for products liability can be based on defective manufacture of a product, defective design of a product, or failure to warn the public of a product's hazards.

Promissory estoppel: An equitable remedy in which the court grants relief to a party who relied to his detriment on the promise of another; see quasi contract.

Promissory note: The written agreement to repay a debt.

Prosecutor: The legal representative for the federal government or a state in a criminal matter; the U.S. attorney, state attorney, or county attorney.

Proxy: A person who speaks for or votes for a corporate shareholder in a meeting.

Purchase money security interest: A security interest that attaches and is automatically perfected because the creditor advances the money to purchase the collateral to the debtor.

Quasi contract: An equitable remedy in which a court grants relief to a party who relied to his detriment on the promise of another; see promissory estoppel.

Reasonable person: In tort law, an imaginary construct representing the standard of conduct that an average, ordinary person would follow in a certain situation. A reasonable person acts sensibly; a reasonable person is not negligent.

Reckless: Thoughtless; failing to act property when one should have known better or should have taken better precautions to avoid a risk of harm.

Record: The transcript from a court trial of a case that contains all the testimony and exhibits given at trial.

Recovery: The amount awarded in a judgment.

Rejection: Declining or turning down an offer.

Repossess: To take an item into one's control to satisfy a past-due obligation.

Rescind: To make void, to annul.

Residence: The county and state in which someone lives for a time.

Respondent: In a lawsuit, the party being sued; the defendant.

Revoke: To take back, to cancel.

Royalty: Money paid to a copyright holder for the sale of his intellectual property.

Secured transaction: A business arrangement in which the buyer gives the seller a promise to repay a debt plus an interest in collateral to guarantee payment of the debt.

Security agreement: The written document between a creditor and a debtor outlining the terms of the debt, the exact collateral pledged, and the circumstances under which the creditor may repossess the collateral to satisfy the debt.

Security interest: The interest that a lender takes in the collateral of the borrower in a secured transaction.

Self-incrimination: Doing or saying something to implicate yourself in a criminal activity. The Fifth Amendment of the U.S. Constitution protects a citizen from being a witness if her testimony may be self-incriminating.

Service contract: A contract between the buyer and seller of goods wherein the seller agrees for a prepaid fee to repair or replace goods covered for a set period of time; sometimes referred to as an extended warranty.

Service mark: A distinctive mark used in the sale of services to identify one's services.

Shrink-wrap agreement: A contract about terms of use put inside the wrapping of a product.

Stakeholder: An individual or group that may have an interest in an endeavor. Corporate stakeholders include the shareholders, employees, business partners, customers, community, and the environment.

Standard of proof: The level or measure of proof required in a trial to determine the guilt of a party.

Stare decisis: Latin phrase which means "let the prior ruling stand." This phrase refers to a court's following of the precedent set by a previous decision in a case with similar circumstances.

Statute of frauds: A contract principle that requires certain types of contracts to be in writing to be enforceable in court.

Strict liability: In tort law, the responsibility for injuries regardless of negligence. Strict liability generally applies to ultrahazardous businesses.

Styled: The legal terminology to refer to a case. The case of a claim between Mr. Marbury and Mr. Madison would be "styled" as *Marbury v. Madison* (the last name of the plaintiff versus the last name of the defendant).

Substantive law: The body of law that creates and defines the rights and duties of citizens.

Surety: A person directly liable to pay another's debt.

Term of art: A word or phrase that has a specific legal meaning; legal jargon.

Tort: In civil law, an injury to a person or property.

Tortfeasor: The person who commits a tort.

Trademark: A distinctive mark or logo attached to goods to identify them with their producer.

Trade secret: A recipe, formula, customer list, price list, or other document owned by a business that is kept secret because of the sensitive and valuable nature of the information.

Trial by combat: A medieval dispute resolution process used by aristocrats involving combat to prove truthfulness; see judicial duel.

Trial by oath: A medieval dispute resolution process whereby the parties to a dispute collected sworn statements from witnesses and character references to prove truthfulness.

Trial by ordeal: A medieval dispute resolution method involving a physical challenge or ordeal to determine truthfulness.

Trier of fact: The person or persons who determine the outcome of a case, either the judge or a jury.

UCC-1: The common form used to file a financing statement.

Unconscionable contract: A contract that is so unfair or one-sided as to offend the conscience of a party. Adhesion contracts, which offer the buyer a "take-it-or-leave-it" deal, are often unconscionable.

Uniform Commercial Code (UCC): A body of rules covering commercial dealings that individual states have adopted to promote uniformity in commerce. Article 2 of the UCC deals with sales of goods. Article 9 of the UCC deals with secured transactions.

Unjust enrichment: Receiving a benefit from another without paying compensation.

Warehouse receipts: Documents showing ownership of goods being held in storage.

Warranty: A promise about the quality or performance of a good for sale that the seller gives to the buyer to induce him to make a purchase.

Warranty for fitness for a specific purpose: A type of guarantee that a seller creates through his words or actions at purchase which gives the buyer a right to expect the product to be suitable for a specific or particular use.

Willful: With intention.

Wrongful death: The tort claim for the unlawful taking of a life.

Index

About the Author

Ellen K. Curry is a Kaplan University professor in the paralegal and business departments, as well as in the Graduate School of Business. She has run a general practice of law for over 25 years in the Iowa and Illinois and has contributed to higher education in the community by instructing in traditional, weekend and online classes at local and national universities. She lives in Davenport, Iowa.